Mental Health Workers' Vicarious Trauma, Secondary Traumatic Stress, and Self-Care

by

Dr. Soraya M. Sawicki, L.C.S.W.

COPYRIGHT 2019©

A Dissertation Presented in Partial Fulfillment of the Requirements for the Degree of Doctor of Social Work, Capella University, January 2019

Author	Dr. Soraya M. Sawicki, L.C.S.W.
Publisher	DBC Publishing, Sandston / Richmond, VA
ISBN-13	978-1948149105
ISBN-10	1948149109
Cover Art	2019© DBC Publishing

This text has been altered in format from the original dissertation to conform to better readability for the general-public and commercial publishing standards. The author may also have updated text, content, added more resources and bibliography material after the original dissertation was first published. Scholars reviewing the contents and formatting for thesis or dissertation styling should _not_ use this book's current *formatting* as a model. Please see your educational institution's established dissertation guidelines for the acceptable formatting for the graduate level thesis for research reporting.

You may contact the author with questions, comments, or continuing research inquiries at: sorayasawicki@aol.com

Abstract

The purpose of this qualitative action research study was to explore mental-health workers' lived experiences when coping with vicarious trauma and how they practice self-care. For the purpose of this study, professional disciplines that make up mental-health workers are licensed social workers, licensed professional counselors, and licensed marriage and family therapists. There is a need to explore this area as the professional and personal well-being of mental-health workers directly impacts service provision.

The research question was: "How do mental-health workers describe coping with vicarious trauma?" The research sub-question was: "How do mental-health workers use self-care in response to vicarious trauma?" The study sample was 12 mental-health workers, from a population of mental-health workers currently working in the field of mental health in a northeastern state. A qualitative transcendental phenomenological approach was incorporated, using semi-structured interviews and a research journal.

Participant demographics were gathered using paper surveys. NVivo 12 was utilized to manage and organize data from the participant transcriptions. The results of the study provided insight of vicarious traumatization and self-care from the perspective of the lived experiences of the mental-health workers not been captured in literature prior to this research study. The four core themes identified were workplace factors, client interactions, stress factors, and self-care factors.

Outcomes indicate mental-health workers are affected at an emotional level, as well as a physical level. The levels may have to do with the length of time in the field, their own personal history of trauma, or their available support systems. There is a disconnect between workers who experience vicarious trauma, their personal self-care, and the meaning of self-care. Recommendations for future research are provided.

Dedication & Acknowledgments

This dissertation is dedicated to my husband, Chet Sawicki, my five children, and my parents. When I say the word family, it comes along with a wide, proud smile, as well as a sense of sadness for the ones no longer here. My husband is the foundation behind all of my work. When I told him I wanted to go after my dream of a DSW degree, he agreed to support me 100%. He ensured I always had everything I needed to succeed – from morning coffee to late-night snacks. He provided pep talks when I was contemplating giving up; he wiped my tears; he gave up his needs to ensure mine were met. Honey, I love you and I will forever be grateful. If it were not for you, I could not have done this; you are 'the wind beneath my wings' – you helped me fly!

To my mother, Maria Reyes, who always told me to go after my dreams, I love you mom. To my father, Rafael Martinez, who is not here to celebrate, but I know he is happy from above. I love you, dad – I told you I would do this. I am a scholar – I have a Doctorate! To my siblings, Ana, Diane, Ralf, and Eddy, and mother-in-law Stephanie, thank you for understanding and forgiving my absences because of school work. My five children are my greatest inspirations, Luis, Stephanie, Chelsea, Steven, and Shane. This accomplishment was not just for me, I achieved it for *you*. I want each one of you to know I hope you never give up on your dreams. If you want it bad enough, you and only you, can make it happen.

I love you all. I am so proud to be your mother.

I would like to say thank you to those who truly believed in me. I want to thank Ms. J.R., without you I could not have finalized this journey. Thank you for your trust, encouragement, and words of wisdom. I will forever be grateful to you. I also want to extend my respect to the 12 mental-health workers that participated in this research study. Thank you for sitting with me for hours while you shared with me your deepest joys and pains. You inspired me and will forever be part of me as part of my journey. Thank you for the time, dedication, and attention you give to the families with whom you work. You are deserving of admiration as you have dedicated your lives to serving individuals with urgent needs despite the inherent risks on your own well-being.

Thank you, Julie, for always being there. You are the true meaning of a friend; thank you for all those words of encouragement. Thank you to my peers for supporting and encouraging me. Thank you, Dr. Looney and Dr. G, for your encouragement and words of wisdom. A special thanks to Dr. Post, for always believing in me.

I would like to thank Capella University for providing a great academic environment. Thank you to my committee, my mentor, Dr. Robin Ersing; you were so patient and understanding as you guided me through this journey. Your expertise and knowledge will always be part of me. To my other team members, Dr. Ruth Ahlman and Dr. Martha Raske; thank you, for your time and expertise. I will always admire your dedication as scholars and instructors.

Dr. Soraya Martinez Sawicki, L.C.S.W.

Table of Contents

List of Tables

Chapter 1

Introduction

Background of the Problem

Vicarious Trauma (VT) is a term used to describe the traumatic exposure to the disturbing experiences of others (Molnar et al., 2017). Secondary Traumatic Stress (STS) and VT are terms frequently used conversely to describe the consequences of secondary traumatic exposure. These experiences may affect service providers in unusual ways, consequently, affecting their everyday work. Secondary traumatic stress is defined as the partaking of disturbing experiences, mainly in situations where the listener is extremely empathic or tries to be, and traumatic symptoms in the listener may be aroused that can be equivalent to those of the victim (Butler, Carello, & Manguin, 2017; Figley,

1999). While the social-work field has been looking deeply at the impact of trauma on clients, little is known of treatment designed for the workers (Sansbury, Graves, & Scott, 2015).

Individuals working in the field of trauma, mental health, police force, fire response, emergency services, and other areas are exposed to distressing daily events (Molnar et al., 2017). These professionals are exposed to victims trauma experiences for years through daily work with their clients. Consequently, vicarious traumatization may develop, can damage or alter the professionals' sense of identity, and harmfully impact their emotional welfare (Hernandez-Wolfe, Killian, Engstrom, & Gangsei, 2015). It is estimated that 24 million or 8% of the US populace will experience a traumatic stress response throughout their lives. Among professionals in the mental-health field, the number is between 15% to 50%, which is possibly six times higher than the average individual (Sansbury et al., 2015). Mental-health professionals are often exposed to a larger amount of distressing experiences raised by their patients (Halevi & Idisis, 2017), resulting in social workers experiencing significant traumatic reactions.

Reactions may be demonstrated by an alteration in sensitive, intellectual, and physical conduct possibly reflective of post-traumatic indications such as invasive memories (recollections), hyper-arousal, avoiding regular circumstances, a surge in relational issues, and a decrease in the pleasure of everyday life (Halevi & Idisis, 2017). The world may appear changed to the worker because of a similar trauma (Sansbury et al., 2015). For example, a worker treating a client with issues of domestic violence who has a personal history of domestic violence may be triggered by the client's present experience, which the social worker may not have addressed in their own past. Mental-health workers have habitually ignored how important it is to pay attention to routine stressors that affect their own work, which makes counseling advice, relayed to their patients, potentially insincere (Dattilio, 2015). A practice of mental-health professionals is to promote wellness and well-being to clients. Mental-health professionals fail to nurture themselves spiritually, emotionally, and psychologically. This 'failure to nurture' issue is now recognized; and professional articles describe the lingering disregard for the self-care of mental-health workers as a professional hindrance (Caringi et al., 2017; Dattilio, 2015; Molnar et al., 2017). Even qualified social- and other mental-health workers, who have experienced trauma and work in challenging situations with individuals and families, are not prepared for traumatic encounters and are negatively affected (Caringi et al., 2017).

Mental-health workers, (e.g., social workers), first responders, and other professional groups work extended hours to aid the most susceptible populations in society, many suffering trauma (Molnar et al., 2017). There is growing attention to the prevalence of trauma and its negative consequences (Sansbury et al., 2015). Traumatic occurrences can distress a person in significant ways, and a mass trauma that distresses a large number of people can have severe repercussions for individuals, the community, and the workers who assist them (Day, Lawson, & Burge, 2017). For example, on April 6th, 2007 there was a mass shooting at Virginia Polytechnic Institute and State University (commonly known as Virginia Tech). The shooting affected the campus population of over 30,000 students, the surrounding community, as well as the first

responders and clinicians (Day et al., 2017). It would
be useful for researchers, educators, policymakers,
organizational and political leaders, to pay attention to
social workers and other professionals in this field.
Without proper consideration, mental-health workers
(e.g., social workers), and other professionals are left
defenseless to the collective (and added) burden of
trauma accumulated from the long-lasting and severe
hardship of VT/STS (Molnar et al., 2017). Often,
social workers who have had their own traumatic
experiences will quietly hide behind denial (Molnar et
al., 2017). A worker may be ashamed of their own
past history of a traumatic event and not sought
services. If not addressed, these professionals may
suffer further damage, resulting in job loss, burnout,
or resignation . Professionals in the social-work field
are encouraged to provide services and move beyond
their unspoken resilience. Resiliency is defined as a
belief that workers have fortés (hidden and/or
professional strengths) to face stress or a
catastrophic event on their own, or by seeking
suitable resources (Molnar et al., 2017).

Educational institutions, educators, mental
health organizations, and policymakers could benefit

in expanding their knowledge of VT- and STS-related issues. Researchers would also benefit from expanding extant investigations in this area of study. The mental welfare of providers is crucial in their capability to perform and deliver appropriate treatment (Caringi et al., 2017). There is a need to explore this area, as the well-being of mental-health professionals directly impacts service provision (Molnar et al., 2017). Not all individuals who closely interacts with a distressed/traumatized individual will experience STS (Ivicic & Motta, 2017).

This action research examined the connection between mental-health workers, how they cope when working with VT, and ways in which these professionals practice self-care. This research study is qualitative, using a phenomenological approach and the constructivist self-development theory as a foundation. Professionals, educational-, and mental-health organizations, could benefit from expanding extant research and treatment of VT/STS.

Constructivist Self-Development Theory

The constructivist self-development theory is
the theoretical configuration for this research study.
McCann and Pearlman's (1990a) Constructivist Self-
Development Theory (CSDT) offers a complete
conceptual framework for comprehending the
vicarious traumatization. In the late 1980s, Pearlman
and Maclan (1995) fused psychoanalytic theories to
develop the CSDT. Pearlman and Maclan (1995)
developed the theory to learn and treat survivors of
traumatic events.

According to McCann and Pearlman (1990a),
the trauma experience originates from exposure to an
extremely upsetting incident or series of events that
can disrupt the person (mentally or emotionally). The
basic principle of CSDT is that people have the
intrinsic capability of creating their own individual
realities as they interrelate those realities or
experiences with their environments (McCann &
Pearlman, 1990a). The response to a trauma is a
multifaceted progression that comprises the
individual's meaning and imageries of the events,
extending to the most profound parts of the

individual's internal understanding of their self, subsequently resulting in exclusive variation (McCann & Pearlman, 1990a). Exclusive variation meaning a change unique to their persona.

When pertaining to the trauma worker, the CSDT theory specifically points out how treating traumatized clients can disturb the counselor's images of recollection, as well as representation about themselves (Dunkey & Whelan, 2006; McCann & Pearlman, 1990b). The term Vicarious Trauma was derived from the CSDT research and the resulting theory. Competent social workers are employed in highly-demanding work environments, often dealing with clients who have experienced the impact of a substantial traumatic experience (Caringi et al., 2017). Even though the social workers have been deemed qualified to work in these tough conditions, they can be adversely affected by the distressing traumatic exposure the client or families may have endured (Caringi et al., 2017). Not all workers will be affected the same way. McMann and Pearlman (1990b) presented the notion of the conveyance of opinions and supposition about the world and how it connects to the distressing experience from the individual to the worker, calling this phenomenon vicarious traumatization (Caringi et al., 2017). This research has increased awareness and encouraged investigations on VT and STS regarding mental-health workers. Secondary Traumatic Stress (STS) denotes the actions and sentiments linked with serving a distressed or anguished individual (Caringi et al., 2017; Figley, 1995).

Phenomenology

Phenomenology is an approach to investigating and capturing an individual's interpretations of beliefs and their understandings of the world (Ellis, 2016). In phenomenology, the researcher uses purposeful sampling to select individuals who have experienced the phenomenon being investigated (Ellis, 2016). Qualitative studies involve the use of fewer participants to answer the research question. Random participants would not benefit a research project based on phenomenology because a researcher cannot assume this individual has experienced the phenomenon being investigated. Research participants are expected to produce

copious, meaningful, rigorous material on the
research question that would permit the researcher to
come up with an extensive account of the
phenomenon (Cleary, Horsfall, & Hayter, 2014). The
type and number of participants chosen would
depend on the knowledge the researcher is
attempting to gain, as well as the purpose, benefits,
and validity of the research study (Cleary et al., 2014).
Different size samples have been suggested for
phenomenological studies, however, a sample of
between six and 20 participants would suffice (Ellis,
2016). Smaller sample sizes are appropriate due to
the concentration of the interviews. A few selection
principles for sample choice in phenomenology
include small numbers of participants, which allow for
more focused and intense investigations and
individuals are chosen purposefully (to answer
specific research questions), instead of predetermined samples, which provides a rationale for
selection (Ellis, 2016). The sample for this study was
12 participants employed as mental-health workers in
a community clinic in a northeastern, United States
state. The potential participants were screened for
VT. If the participants in the sample pool fit the

inclusion criteria, they moved on to participate in the study.

Statement of the Problem

The research problem is identified as being mental-health workers (e.g., social workers) that experience VT through daily work, and rarely practice self-care (Pakenham, 2015; Tavormina, & Clossey, 2015). Individuals employed in the field of victim support, mental health, the police force, fire response, emergency facilities, and other specialties, experience traumatic occurrences daily (Molnar et al., 2017). These events may affect service providers in unusual ways, potentially impacting their effectiveness as mental-health practitioners in negative or detrimental ways.

Purpose of the Study

The purpose of this qualitative research study was to explore mental health worker's experiences of coping with VT, and how mental-health workers incorporate self-care while working in a community, mental-health clinic in a northeastern state. Self-care approaches include seeking personal therapy, taking time for personal relationships, making changes in their everyday lives, and being involved in external and internal organizational events (Zahniser, Rupert, & Dorociak, 2017).

The goals of this research study were to establish ongoing self-care initiatives, to use training and curriculum to improve the quality of health and well-being for mental-health workers at employment worksites, and to create a culture of self-care within the work environment. For this investigation, qualified mental-health workers may include any of the following: social workers, licensed social workers, licensed professional counselors, licensed marriage and family therapists, and bachelor-level social workers. This research project, follow-on training, and curriculum presentation may result in job retention and a decrease in staff turnover within this specific mental-health clinic.

Significance of the Study

This research study was focused on enhancing the social-work profession by exploring the effects of VT on the overall daily experience of the professionals in the field. It would benefit society as a whole as professionals in the field are on the forefront when tragedy occurs. By exploring daily experiences of mental-healthcare workers, strategies may be developed to help these professionals when they are personally dealing with distressing situations or working with clients whose situations may trigger VT or STS. Social-work professionals need to manage daily challenges that affect them professionally and personally (Hernandez-Wolfe et al., 2015). It is imperative these issues be addressed to establish best practices for future mental-health professionals. It will be beneficial to start with the education of future social workers in areas such as prevention, management, and awareness when dealing with this phenomenon.

Investigations on the effects of VT on the overall daily experience would provide professionals, educators, and mental-health and social-work organizations an opportunity to examine experiences of individuals exhibiting the phenomenon. The outcomes of this research study can provide tools to manage daily experiences that may cause internal turmoil or feelings of inadequacy (for the mental-health professionals or first-responders). Vicarious trauma denotes the accrued effects of treating distressed clients, which involves intrusion of the worker's feelings, intellectual schematics and recollections, self-efficacy, and sense of well-being (Dorociak et al., 2017). Vicarious trauma does not produce illness in the worker or the victim, it is the conveyance of distress by being exposed to troubling clinical material (Hernandez-Wolfe et al., 2015). Mental-health professionals are exposed to VT daily. There has been heightened awareness in the significance of self-care for mental-health workers (Dorociak et al., 2017).

Practicing mental-health professionals face countless stressors that must be managed to function optimally in the workplace and their daily lives (Dorociak et al., 2017). These stressors may cause increased work-related pressure that, if not addressed, may have undesirable consequences on the mental-health professional's ability to provide mental-health services to their clients. Stress can be an occupational hazard when delivering services to traumatized individuals. This can become a health risk, threatening the labor force both personally and professionally (Molnar et al., 2017). When social workers and other professionals deal with stress, in the absence of effective coping, anguish will often be followed by distress and agony (Dorociak et al., 2017). Stress, lack of self-care, and the absence of a culture-of-care within a working organization can be detrimental to counseling and social-work professionals. Without a combined effort from researchers, political and organizational leaders, these professional mental-health individuals are left vulnerable to the collective weight of VT and STS (Molnar et al., 2017).

The impact this study will have on the site location will be beneficial to the workers, the work environment, the population, and the clients served. To provide beneficial treatment to clients, workers need to be mentally and physically healthy. Self-care needs to be implemented in work settings. According to Dorociak et al. (2017), when workers are mentally and physically healthy, outcomes are positive. Preliminary research studies indicate self-care is related to professional well-being and outcomes (Dorociak et al., 2017). The social-work profession holds high regard to provision of services. The importance of service provision is instilled in every social worker and stated in the profession's code of ethics. The social worker's primary goals are to aid people in need, focus on social issues, and provide service to others beyond self-interest (National Association of Social Workers [NASW], 2017; Wheeler & McClain, 2015). Special attention should be directed at service providers since these workers are the individuals dealing directly with trauma victims. Beyond preventing problems, practical and constant self-care enhances overall well-being, therefore contributing to an optimal level of professional performance (Dorociak, et al., 2017).

Research Design

This action-research study examined the connection between mental-health workers, how they coped when working with VT, and how they practiced self-care. This study is qualitative, using a transcendental-phenomenological approach. The research problem identified was that mental-health workers experience VT through daily work and seldom practice self-care. The research study involved VT, also known as Secondary Traumatic Stress (STS). This is secondary trauma experienced by helping professionals, due to hearing accounts of harmful experiences shared by their patients. This research study's target population is mental-health workers employed in a community mental-health clinic in a northeastern state. This study employs 12 participants currently working in the mental-health field.

The Secondary Traumatic Stress Scale (STSS) was utilized to identify secondary traumatic symptoms, and also served as a qualifier. To be part of the study, potential participants had to score a 28 or above on the STSS. Data collection included a paper survey to collect participant's demographics: gender, age, length of time working at the current agency, and length of years employed as a mental-health worker, in-depth interviews with open-ended questions, and the researcher's journal. Through

collective lived experiences described by the subjects,
patterns and themes were identified and established.
Interviews were conducted in a safe space and
transcribed. A field journal was used to document
and create an audit trail as a supplement to data
collection. Triangulation was achieved by gathering
generated data from the descriptive analysis, the
STSS, interviews, and the researcher's journal. The
following is more detailed description of data
collection methods.

The Secondary Traumatic Screening Scale

The STSS (Bride, 2007) is used to measure
the subject's responses to VT. The STSS was the
screening tool used for identifying individuals with VT.
The STSS (Bride, Robinson, Yegidis, & Figley, 2004)
is a 17-entry instrument using self-reporting methods,
intended to measure the incidence of intrusion,
avoidance, and arousal pointers related with STS
(Bride, 2007). Prospective participants responded
using a five-point Likert scale. The Likert scale
included responses ranging from *never* to *very often*.
These choices allowed them to indicate their feelings

within the past week. The STSS covers three subscales: Intrusion, Avoidance, and Arousal. An
intrusive thought is an unwelcomed involuntary
thought, image, or idea. Avoidance would be the act
of choosing one's own behavior based on trying to
avoid or escape a situation, specific thoughts, or
feelings. Arousal is the external response to internal
or external stimuli. The phrasing of detailed stressor
items is intended so the traumatic stressor is known
as an experience to clients (Bride, 2007). The data
gathered from the STSS was used as a threshold to
identify those who scored the 28 as opposed to those
who did not. The interviews and journal provided
qualitative data used to identify patterns and themes.
The patterns and themes were reviewed by the
researcher for interpretation and meaning. The STSS
was established because instruments were needed to
measure STS/VT indicators precisely in social
workers and other 'helping' specialists (Bride et al.,
2004).

Secondary Traumatic Stress Scale Psychometrics

The STSS has verified evidence of convergent, discriminant, factorial validity, and high levels of internal consistency (Bride, 2007; Bride et al., 2004). The instrument can be used to commence empirical investigations into the prevention and improvement of STS among practitioners (Bride et al., 2004). Coefficient alpha was used to assess internal consistency. Means, standard deviations, and alpha levels for the STSS and subscales were as indicated, Full STSS (M = 29.49, SD = 10.76, α = .93), Intrusion (M = 8.11, SD = 3.03, α = .80), Avoidance (M = 12.49, SD = 5.0, α = .87) and Arousal (M = 8.89, SD = 3.57, α = .83). Alpha levels between .80 and .90 should be considered great (Bride et al., 2004). The Bonferroni technique was used to set the family-wise error rate at α = .05 resulting in a per comparison alpha level of .00179 (.05/28; (because 28 correlations were prearranged when examining convergent and discriminant validity) (Bride et al., 2004). The factorial legitimacy of the STSS was addressed using confirmatory factor analysis using structural equation modeling SEM techniques and the extreme likelihood estimation (Bride et al., 2004). LISREL 8.3 software was used for the analysis through a covariance medium (Bride et al., 2004).

Interviews

Participants were scheduled to be part of an in-depth interview which was recorded and transcribed. Participants were asked to answer 10 open-ended questions to the best of their ability. The interviews were tape recorded and conducted in a safe and confidential space. Patterns and themes were identified from the data collected. These patterns and themes revealed data that addressed the research questions. The in-depth interviews generated qualitative data. The data were analyzed using NVivo software and the transcendental-phenomenological approach was used for interpretation.

The interview questions were developed specifically for this research investigation and were field tested by experts. Using open-ended questions allowed all the subjects to answer subjectively without using one-word responses. Subjects shared personal experiences as rapport was established with the researcher. Semi-structured interviews incorporate the use of pre-arranged questions; the investigator asks clarifying questions with the purpose of gathering comparable types of topic data from the subjects, creating a feeling of research and theory direction (Doody & Noonan, 2013). The interview was flexible with open-ended questions, allowing discussion and exploration of issues that arose as the interview progressed. The interview process began with easy questions which made the participants feel comfortable while providing essential information. The researcher is then able to move on to more delicate topics (Doody & Noonan, 2013). In qualitative research, the investigator's goals are to comprehend people's lived experiences (Doody & Noonan, 2013). Questions in the interview are rich, neutral and delicate (Doody & Noonan, 2013). Questions can be based on actions, experiences, opinions, worth, moods, facts, sensory experiences, demographics, or background details (Doody & Noonan, 2013). The interview questions are devised to get the best possible answers to support or dispute the researcher's stated theory.

Journal

When conducting qualitative research, data can be gathered in a variety of ways, to include obtaining documentary data (McNiff, 2017). Some documentary-data examples are logs, diaries, and journals. Researchers may utilize any of these methods to record a particular act, personal reflections, and the knowledge from which it stems (McNiff, 2017). While conducting this research investigation, a journal was retained, which included all phases of the planning, implementation, and organization of the research project. In addition to notes of interview issues that arose, self-reflection was also an integral part of the journal. This information was transcribed, as the journal was the third-data source. The journal generated qualitative data, which was also analyzed using NVivo 12.

Target study participants' inclusion criteria were comprised of employment at the clinic in the capacity of mental-health worker, either by licensure or job description, (licensed-professional counselors, licensed master's social workers, licensed-clinical social workers, social workers, family coordinators, and/or intake workers). Further inclusion criteria were a score of 28 or above on the STSS, an age of greater than 18, and residency in the applicable state. Participants included both genders. Exclusion criteria included anyone with an active *Diagnostic Statistical Manual* (5th ed.) diagnosis, students, and/or volunteers at the community clinic, and a score below 28 on the STSS Research Questions.

The Research Question

A research question is the central core of a research study. The research question for this research study is: "How do mental-health workers describe coping with vicarious trauma?" The research sub-question is: "How do mental-health workers use self-care in response to vicarious trauma?"

Assumptions and Limitations

An assumption in research refers to a statement considered true, although it has not been proven. According to Kirkwood and Price (2013), the researcher's views and assumptions outline the

research they undertake. There are three
assumptions in this investigation. The first
assumption is that participants would be honest when
answering the research questions; confidentiality
would be in place, so names and place of
employment would be anonymous; and subjects
would participate voluntarily (they could remove
themselves from the study at any time without
penalty). The second assumption was each person's
reality is different, therefore affecting patterns and
themes. The open-ended and in-depth interview
questions were devised in such a way that
participants could describe lived experiences, thus
questions were utilized to identify those similar
patterns and themes. The third assumption was
participants would score high on the STSS due to
work and lived experiences in the field.

For phenomenology investigations to be
trustworthy, process documentation must be
established. This process includes choice of the
topic, stages of data gathering, data analysis, and the
creation of an indispensable description of the
phenomenon (Donalek, 2004). Phenomenology
investigations are used when there is little known

about the issue, or when there is delicate content (Donalek, 2004). For researchers to have a successful and truthful interview, researchers need to be engaged and sensitive. It was predicted that participants will have different feedback, depending on their own realities and perceptions, therefore yielding a variety of patterns and themes. The goal of an investigation is to get an indispensable and in-depth description of the phenomenon (Donalek, 2004).

Limitations in research are influences beyond the researcher's control. Limitations may restrict the outcomes expected by the researcher. There were three-key limitations to this study. The first limitation was this study does not take the (years of) experience of the participants into account when selecting participants for the study. It is possible participants' inexperience might impact their reporting of any VT. The second limitation was that better outcomes and understanding of VT may possibly have been obtained if a different methodology was used. The third limitation was the majority of study participants were females, which excluded a gendered-balance of experiences from the male perspective.

There may be certain healthcare professionals more exposed to VT more than others. Licensed clinical social workers may be exposed more than licensed masters' social workers due to licensing (credentials and qualifications). Another limitation was not including administrative staff (clients may have shared information with them). In future studies, it may be beneficial to academic research to include non-clinical, office staff.

This investigation incorporated a phenomenological approach. The subjects were better able to answer the research questions; therefore, a different research (methodology) would not have been beneficial. If a different approach (or method) were used, it would not be helpful to the subjects. Some of the target population in the study may not have been exposed to the benefits and education of self-care in the field. Another area of potential improvement would be the inclusion of males in the study. This would require conducting the same study at another site with more male workers to obtain additional male perspectives. Although males and females were invited to participate, the researcher was unable to control the ratio of females to males in this research study based on access to the population group.

There are limitations in all research studies. These limitations may impact any research study as qualitative studies use a smaller sample size resulting in difficulties to generalize the results of the smaller study group to the larger population. This study could have been conducted using two or more mental health agencies and comparing the data outcomes. Qualitative data requires less subjects than quantitative data, therefore, the recommendations for future research may be to carry out a quantitative or mixed-method investigation with a larger sample size. If this research study had been based on a larger sample size, the results may have been more applicable to the general population. Steps were taken to minimize limitations; however, certain limitations in research are innate (Bride, 2007).

Definition of Terms

The following definition of terms will aid in understanding how the research questions have been answered. For this study, VT and STS have been used to describe symptoms and behaviors associated with vicarious traumatization.

Secondary Traumatic Stress (STS), represents behaviors and emotions after aiding a traumatized or pained individual (Caringi et al., 2017; Fingley, 1995).

Self-care is defined as an intricate, all-purpose process of the deliberate undertaking of approaches that bolster healthy performance and reinforce wellness through activities such as, pursuing therapy, spending time with loved ones, making changes in the employment setting, and taking an active part in fun filled events (Dorociak et al., 2017).

Vicarious trauma (VT) denotes the accrued consequence of working with distressed individuals, it involves intrusion of the workers feelings, intellectual schemas and recollections, self-efficacy, and intrusion on overall well-being (Dorociak et al., 2017).

Expected Findings

This study was geared at enhancing the mental-health profession by identifying VT and secondary stress in the everyday lived experience of mental-health workers – specifically social workers. It was expected that additional support would be needed in the field when working with traumatized individuals. By investigating the effects of VT on the overall daily experience, professionals in the mental-health field could be better equipped to manage work-related stress (for themselves), which may cause internal turmoil or feelings of inadequacy. Vicarious trauma is when the accrued effects of treating traumatized clients, interferes with the worker's feelings, intellectual schemas and recollections, and the feelings of being unsafe (Dorociak et al., 2017). Vicarious trauma does not symbolize illness in the worker or the client; it is the passing on of traumatic stress by listening to distressing information from clients or others (Hernandez-Wolf et al., 2015). Mental-health professionals are exposed to VT daily. In recent years, the importance of self-care for mental-health workers has increased due to

recognized instances of VT/STS (Dorociak et al.,
2017).

Practicing mental-health professionals face
demands that must be managed to perform effectively
in the job, for their clients, and in their everyday
business and private lives. These stresses may
cause great anxiety that, if not taken care of, can
possibly have adverse consequences for service
provision. Occupational threats for providing services
to traumatized and violence exposed individuals can
become a public-health hazard, threatening workers'
mental and emotional equilibrium (Molnar et al.,
2017). This progression of work-related stress has
been compared to a descending journey that begins
when stress is not handled properly and leads to
anguish in the worker (Dorociak et al., 2017). Stress,
lack of self-care, and the absence of a culture-of-care
within a work organization can be detrimental to the
workers in counseling- and social-work professions.
Without a coordinated effort from researchers,
political and community leaders, and agency
administrators, mental-health professionals will be
vulnerable to the accumulating load of VT and STS
(Molnar et al., 2017).

The expectations for this project were results from the collected data would answer the research questions, the outcomes and data conclusions would reflect levels of VT/STS among the mental-health workers, and recommendations would indicate the need for self-care initiatives within any mental-health provider organization. The impact of this study on the worksite location will benefit the clinical work environment, the professional employee population, and clients served in a mental-health capacity. It is unrealistic to expect mental-health workers to be healthy 100% of the time; clinics do expect their mental health providers to be functional enough to complete their work and provide effective services to their clients.

Consideration needs to be given when providing beneficial treatment to clients, which requires the worker to be mentally healthy. Self-care needs to be implemented in work settings to provide mental-health workers with additional tools to support work-related stress. According to Dorociak et al. (2017), when workers are healthy, treatment outcomes are positive. Preliminary studies indicate self-care is linked to professional well-being and outcomes (Dorociak et al., 2017). Service provision is instilled in social workers that clients are a priority. As stated in the profession's code of ethics, the social workers main purpose is to aid vulnerable individuals, address social issues, and provide service to others while disregarding self-interest (NASW, 2017; Wheeler & McClain, 2015).

Special attention should be directed to service providers since they are the professionals expected to provide qualified services to their clients in need. Beyond preventing problems, hands-on and continuous self-care improves functioning and general well-being to the mental-health professionals' clients, which in turn contributes to an increased level of professional performance (Dorociak et al., 2017). The expected findings of this study have aligned with the goal of this investigation – to establish ongoing self-care monitoring in the workplace environment in response to VT and STS. The conclusions and recommendations of this research study were expected to reflect a need for training and an enhanced curriculum to improve the quality of health and well-being for the mental-health workers while creating a culture of care within the organization.

Chapter 2

Literature Review

Introduction

The following literature review was conducted for VT (STS) in the field of mental health. This chapter addresses five specific areas: a discussion on the theoretical framework, a review of the literature, a synthesis of the results in the literature review, a critique of the research methods and procedures, and a summary. The literature review shows a path towards understanding VT and the underpinnings associated with it, while addressing a gap in self-care and treatment of mental-health workers experiencing VT. While mental-health workers prioritize the well-being of clients, there seems to be a disconnect between workers' feelings and behaviors after working with traumatized individuals.

It would be a benefit to professionals,

academics, policymakers, and institutions that researchers continue to elaborate on mental-health workers' VY and self-care. This action-research study examined the connection between mental-health workers, how they cope when working with VT, and ways in which they practice self-care. Vicarious Trauma is the concept that defines the psychological consequences of working with traumatic individuals. Secondary traumatic experience defines the behaviors of these same individuals. Older studies were included to identify how this issue has been, and continues to be, a work in progress.

Theoretical Orientation for the Study

The constructivist self-development theory (CSDT) offered the theoretic backbone for the current study. A theory is like a map and is used to provide a framework for investigation. It is used to provide a way of understanding pieces of human experience which may otherwise seem unrelated (McCann & Pearlman, 1990a). In the late 1980s, Pearlman and Maclan (1995) merged psychoanalytic theories to develop the CSDT theory to study and treat survivors of traumatic events.

According to McCann and Pearlman (1990a), the trauma experience begins with exposure to extremely distressing incident or sequence of events that can disrupt the self. The fundamental principle of CSDT is that people have the intrinsic capability of building their realities as they interrelate with environments (McCann & Pearlman, 1990a). The response to trauma is a complicated course comprised of the individual's meaning and imageries of the events extending to the most profound parts of the individual's internal experience of identity, resulting in unique a transformation (McCann & Pearlman, 1990a).

Saakvitne, Tennen, and Affleck (1998) state that CSDT describes character growth as the interface among a central capability linked to primary relations, safe attachments, ego resources, as well as the created opinions and views related to accumulated experiences. These experiences could be related to earlier traumatic events. Since CSDT points out aspects of development affected by trauma, it can be considered a clinical-trauma theory (McCann & Pearlman, 1990a). Saakvitne et al.

(1998) described how the theorist developed CSDT utilizing clinical and untried data from trauma groups.

Pearlman and Maclan (1995) carried out a quantitative study incorporating 188 self-identified trauma workers (who helped others) as participants in the New England area and used CSDT as the theoretical framework for their study. The purpose of their study was to investigate the relationship between features of trauma therapy, features of the therapist, and the therapist's psychological performance. This study was the first to measure vicarious traumatization (Pearlman & Maclan, 1995). Vicarious traumatization is the emerging change within the worker due to the empathic interaction with the patient's disturbing experience (Pearlman & Maclan, 1995). The workers completed questionnaires about their experience when working with survivor clients. Using the TSI-brief scale, the researchers found the workers newest in the career field were dealing with the most emotional difficulties.

Pearlman and Maclan (1995) also discovered workers with individual-trauma histories demonstrated increased negative effects from work as opposed to those without a personal history; however, it also showed that trauma work affected those without a history of personal trauma in areas such as self-esteem. Pearlman and Maclan found therapists working longer without a trauma history dealt with increased disturbances in intimacy and self-esteem; this might have been because the workers were utilizing their own therapist to converse about the effect their work had on them (Pearlman & Maclan, 1995). The authors concluded mental-health workers who worked with trauma survivors needed supportive, confidential, and professional relationships to channel the horrifying stories, explicit imageries, and damaging re-creations lived by their clients. Studies by Dombo and Gray (2013); Mairean and Turliuc (2013); and Pearlman, Saakvitne, and Buchele (1995) show individuals working in the 'helping professions,' including first responders, medical doctors, and those in contact with clients' first-hand accounts of traumatic experiences, may be at risk for vicarious traumatization.

Mairean and Turliuc (2013) conducted a quantitative investigation to explore VT when treating human suffering in hospitals in Romania. Specifically, the researchers wanted to explore character alterations in VT views and the interactive properties of character and dealing with these views. A population sample of 131 medical students completed surveys related to personality, coping, and traumatic beliefs. The researchers used regression analysis to emphasize the importance of personality traits as predictors of dysfunctional beliefs. The personality traits included extraversion, neuroticism, and consciousness. The researchers used the CSDT for the theoretical foundation. The researchers hypothesized first that there would be variances between emergency and non-emergency staff in VT. A second hypothesis was the interactions between personality traits and conscious coping would predict participants beliefs. The results supported both hypotheses. This study led to more studies focused on the psychological, professional, and personal consequences of vicarious traumatization on the helping professions (Mairean & Turliuc, 2013). Vicarious trauma can affect any professional that interacts with a survivor client – it does not discriminate between professionals.

Vicarious Trauma and the CSDT

McCann and Pearlman (1990a) devised the phrase vicarious traumatization, which they abstracted from the CSDT (CSDT; McCann & Pearlman, 1990a; Pearlman et al, 1995b). The phenomenon of VT is understood to be the exposure of traumatic material from the client to the therapist. McCann and Pearlman (1990a) stated VT may occur when clients share damaging and graphic material that may alter the worker's unique intellectual schemas, outlooks, and expectations about themselves and others. Vicarious trauma is unique to everyone based on the interaction within the situation and the traumatic event.

Vicarious trauma refers to the absorption of trauma-survivor experiences, sentiments, and responses by professionals interacting with them in the healing process (Dombo & Gray, 2013; Pearlman et al., 1995). Vicarious trauma occurs when the patient or client's traumatic experience affects mental-health workers, co-workers, family members or bystanders in the same manner as it does the victim (McCann & Pearlman, 1990a; Yazdani & Shafi, 2014).

The extent and intensity of the traumatic stories adversely affects or damages others similar to the effect of the experience on the client (Bell & Robinson, 2013). It is not surprising that mental-health workers and other helping professionals would be affected by their line of work in assisting their clients. Due to awareness that treatment and trauma work comes at a cost for mental-health workers who deliver assistance, there has been increased attention in the studies related to the emotional implications of treating individuals who have had traumatic encounters and the ramifications it has on the helping professional (Hyatt-Burkhart, 2014). Vicarious trauma does not always occur. If VT does occur, it is believed to occur (and have affects) over time. Vicarious trauma affects the worker's professional and personal life.

Working with trauma may affect the helping professional and the effects of encountering their client's trauma can affect workers personal lives. The indications of VT fall into four categories which include intrusive imagery, avoidance behaviors, arousal, and changes to the cognitive schemas (Bride, 2007). In intrusive imagery, the individual may experience unwanted recurring thoughts, images, or nightmares. In avoidance, the individual may experience social withdrawal, work absenteeism, evading distressed clients, providing inappropriate treatment (to avoid more revelations from the clients), involvement in negative coping skills or leaving their place of employment. In arousal hypersensitivity, there may be issues concerning safety and emotional effects and/or physical aversion of intimacy. There would also be potential changes in cognitive schemas such as pessimism, cynicism, negativity in spiritual beliefs and a different view of the world (Branson, Weigand, & Keller, 2014; Bride et al., 2004; McCann & Pearlman, 1990a; Pryce, Shackelford, & Pryce, 2007).

In a quantitative study conducted by Branson et al. (2014), the researchers examined the association among VT and sexual longing, using the constructivist self-development theory as a foundational framework. The researchers had a study population sample of 163 volunteers from the Missouri Substance abuse Professional Credentialing Board (MSAPCB). The researchers felt there was a gap in the literature concerning the negative consequences of VT on mental-health professionals, specifically related to aversion in the personal area. Branson et al. (2014) stated that in the areas of aversion, private matters would not be discussed willingly with supervisors, co-workers, or professors. The trademark of VT in therapists/behavioral health workers is a negative change in the cognitive schema (McCann & Pearlman, 1990b). Mental-health workers dealing with VT might not feel comfortable in disclosing personal concerns (Branson et al., 2014).

The researchers had two experimental hypotheses. The first hypothesis was, it was expected there would be an antipathy association between experiences of VT and the level of sexual longing between the behavioral-health workers. The second hypothesis was levels of VT were expected to predict levels of sexual longing over and above the influence of the four covariates identified as years of professional experience, sexual trauma history, age and gender (Branson et al., 2014). Data was gathered through online surveys. Individuals who were retired, non-clinical, or not sexually active were excluded. Additional data was gathered using the STSS to look at indications of avoidance, intrusion, and arousal, which is used to measure therapist struggling with negative reactions to the traumatic material (Bride, 2007). The Hubert Index of Sexual Desire measured the level of a participant's sexual desire; a demographic questionnaire was used to collect basic demographics.

The researchers found a noteworthy inverse connection between VT and sexual longing. As the numbers due to VT increased, the numbers of sexual longing decreased (Branson et al., 2014). Vicarious trauma was found to be a pointedly tougher predictor of sexual longing than the other four covariates. Age, gender, history of sexual trauma, or professional experience came second to vicarious traumatization. The researchers made an important statement by stating that behavioral-health clinicians struggling with VT need to have a better understanding of their symptoms to decrease or prevent further negative consequences (Branson et al., 2014). Listening to a client's revelations of disturbing events affects the behavioral-health clinician's interpretation of the world, their frame of reference, and their own feeling of safety by fighting and shifting their inner intellectual schema (Branson et al., 2014; Dunkley & Whelan,

2006). This research was a relevant example of how VT may affect mental-health professionals in personal aspects, especially in the area related to aversion. Not everyone will be affected by VT. It is believed some individuals may even experience a certain amount of vicarious resilience as shown in the next study.

Vicarious trauma has negative consequences on the treating provider, the symptoms almost mimic the symptoms being experienced by the victim; however, VT may affect the professional worker depending on their own history of trauma, support system, and individual differences. For example, Hernandez-Wolfe et al. (2015) explored the association among vicarious traumatization and vicarious resilience and looked at the possibility of the coexistence. Hernandez-Wolfe et al. (2015) conducted a qualitative study to explore the co-existence of vicarious resilience and VT in trauma work with victims of torture in special programs around the USA using a constructivist framework. Hernandez-Wolf et al. (2015) defined vicarious resilience as a concept that aids in interpreting the way in which mental-health workers can be

susceptible to being influenced in a positive way by
the demonstration of resilience exhibited by the
client/victim. The participants were 13 mental-health
workers that worked at treatment centers situated in
the West, East, and Midwest parts of the United
States. The researchers gathered data by conducting
semi-structured interviews, which were audio-taped
and then transcribed. The criterion for selection
required the participants to provide direct service to
survivors and have the suitable credentials, being
social workers, psychologists, and/or marriage and
family therapists (Hernandez-Wolfe et al., 2015).

Researchers found it believable to assume
both positive and negative psychological processes
due to interactions with traumatized individuals.
Trauma workers can be theoretically altered by their
client's trauma and inner strength in positive ways,
even though they may not be totally unencumbered of
distress (Hernandez-Wolfe et al., 2015). At the
clinical level, Hernandez Wolfe et al. (2015) found
attention to VT in training and supervision would
prevent burnout and instill a sense of personal
optimism for the therapist treating the client. Although
vicarious resilience can be experienced by some

workers, VT cannot be prevented from occurring to others. Vicarious trauma can affect individuals according to the environment in which they work as well. Since there are health professionals internationally, workers can be traumatized not only by the experiences shared by their clients, but also by the area where they work.

Finklestein, Stein, Greene, Bronstein, and Solomon (2015) conducted a quantitative study to investigate post-traumatic stress disorder (PTSD) and VT indications between mental-health professionals (MHPs) employed in groups exposed to high levels of trauma from rocket attacks in the Gaza Strip (Palestine). The Gaza Strip is a 40-km strip of land in the Southern Mediterranean. It serves as a 10-km wide border between Egypt and Israel. The sample included 99 mental health professionals (MHPs). The participants completed questionnaires to measure professional support, efficacy, and exposure. Socio-demographic data and post-traumatic stress self-reporting questionnaires were used to collect data. Post-traumatic stress disorder (PTSD) was measured using the PTSD inventory. The researchers examined the association between specialized

supports and sense of self-efficacy with MHP's PTSD
and VT.

The researchers found MHPs employed in the
community of Sderot, a geographic area brutalized by
rocket attacks (2004 - 2014) that resulted in clients
and mental-health professionals having more
personal- and job-related exposure to VT, and higher
levels of PTSD and VT symptoms, as opposed to
mental-health professionals at other Gaza-bordering
communities. Researchers found in vulnerable or
repeated natural-disaster areas, workers are exposed
not only to VT, but also to primary and ongoing
trauma. The researchers specified that mental-health
professionals who have been in their roles for years,
needed additional, supportive supervision and ways
to augment their work-related, self-efficacy to intensify
their resilience (Finklestein et al., 2015). Vicarious
trauma may affect workers and cause STS, and may
also be a recurring phenomenon based on where and
at what capacity the worker is employed.

Vicarious trauma may affect anyone who works
with a client and listens to accounts of disturbing
information. Vicarious trauma can affect individuals
working in different capacities and work locations as

described in the study conducted by Finklestein et al. (2015) in the Gaza Strip. Vicarious trauma has other consequences in addition to the place of work and the role of the worker as described in the next study. Middleton and Potter (2015) conducted a quantitative study of 1,192 child-welfare professionals working in five different child-welfare agencies across four states to examine the link between VT and staff turnover. The researchers used the propositions of the constructivist self-development theory to explore a possible correlation amid VT and the child welfare professionals' intentions to abandon the agency (Middleton & Potter, 2015). The research question was, "What was the causal association between vicarious traumatization and turnover among child-welfare workers?"

Data was collected using a web based or paper survey, and the Comprehensive Organizational Health Assessment (COHA) instrument. The COHA was comprised of numerical data collected in person and online. The study sites included one state-administered, community child-welfare agency located in a Southern state, two county-administered child-welfare agencies located in two different

Midwestern states, and two (Native American) Tribal child-welfare workers in an upper Midwestern state (Middleton & Potter, 2015). The COHA contains 300 questions that measures individual emotional risk and protecting factors in residential and organizational environments and cultural areas. To investigate the association between VT and workforce outcomes, a vicarious-trauma traumatization tool was created and inserted into the 300-item COHA instrument (Middleton & Potter, 2015). Key results of the study highlighted vicarious traumatization as one of the main reasons why child-welfare workers may leave their job; concluding that deterrence and intervention strategies geared at the prevention of vicarious traumatization may help improve the work setting and decrease staff turnover (Middleton & Potter, 2015). It is important to review not only the damage that VT can have on the worker, but also on the service delivery and turnover rates not related to worker role, place of employment, or setting of employment. Vicarious trauma levels and the resulting negative consequences may be associated with different factors.

McCormack and Adams (2016) conducted a qualitative-phenomenological study to explore the subjective interpretations of four, senior, trauma workers working in a clinical setting. Data from semi-structured interviews were analyzed using interpretive phenomenological analysis. The results showed how an individual worker may redefine their own vicarious exposure to trauma as personal and psychological growth. According to McCormack and Adams (2016), the study opens an opportunity to look at the interpersonal relationships of therapists and clients, highlighting the potential for both VT and psychological growth. The results enhanced the research study results of Hernandez-Wolfe et al. (2015) who suggested there can be individual benefits and positive changes as a result of vicarious exposure. McCormack and Adams (2016) mentioned that – without the right organizational support – a therapist in inpatient settings may be in danger of poor self-actualization. Therapists without organizational support may experience long-lasting psychopathology as they struggle to make sense of their anguish from VT exposure. This may be reflected in their ability to combine (or separate) their personal and professional identities. VT causes a powerful transformation on the therapist's inner world, inclusive of schemas, beliefs, and values, leading to lasting psychological and emotional variation (McCormack & Adams, 2016; Pearlman & Saakvitne, 1995a).

According to Boulanger (2016), trauma is infectious. In some cases, sharing difficult narratives with disturbing information carries a risk of vicarious contamination of the mental-health worker (McCormack & Adams, 2016). In a qualitative study conducted by Halevi and Idisis (2017), the researchers attempted to predict VT among therapists. The authors incorporated the Bowen's family-systems theory, with a special focus on the phenomenon of differentiation of self. According to Halevi and Idisis, (2017), exposure to the trauma experienced by patients puts the therapist at risk – not only to VT – but also to STS. The researchers incorporated a research-study sample population of 134 therapists who worked in community and private settings. The counselors finished a sequence of questionnaires to gather data pertaining to demographics, differentiation of self, and a belief

scale measuring the presence of VT. The
researchers found an undesirable association
between VT and differentiation of self. Member age
and involvement with treatment were associated with
the differentiation of self and VT (Halevi & Idisis,
2017). The study failed to examine preceding
distressing experiences among the subjects, which
may have impacted the association between vicarious
traumatization and the differentiation of self.
Pearlman and Maclan (1995) established therapists
who had undergone previous trauma were at a higher
jeopardy of developing VT because of increased
susceptibility. Vicarious trauma suggests changes in
the worker's continued ways in how they feel and
view themselves, others, and the world (Edelkott,
Engstrom, Hernandez-Wolfe, & Gangsei, 2016;
Pearlman & Maclan, 1995; Shively, 2017).

Secondary Traumatic Stress

Although the purpose of this research was not
to investigate STS itself, it would be rare when
discussing VT that STS is not mentioned. Since both
terms are similar, it does merit its own section due to

the ways in which the terms are used. Vicarious traumatization involves the intense changes to a professional's intellectual schematics and rooted opinions about self, others and the world, that is a consequence of having been exposed to graphic and/or distressing information involving their client's occurrences (Middleton & Potter, 2015).

Secondary Traumatic Stress denotes a group of symptoms (i.e., behaviors) that imitate PTSD, assimilated through experiences of the individuals who have experienced trauma (Bride & Kintzle, 2011; Figley, 1995; Middleton & Potter, 2015). Although related, STS and PTSD are different concepts. In severe cases, STS may warrant a diagnosis of PTSD (Bride & Kintzle, 2011). While STS mimics symptoms of PTSD, PTSD results from being directly impacted by a disturbing event. Secondary traumatic stress is the consequence of an indirect exposure to trauma because a person comes in contact with the trauma victim (Rzeszutek, Partyka, & Golab, 2015). Secondary traumatic stress is vicarious and transmitted as a result of listening to tragic information.

Both STS and VT can play an undesirable role in service provision. Symptoms of STS can impact healthcare professionals and the treatment they provide (Rzeszutek et al., 2015). For example, mental-health workers and other professionals (e.g., social workers) may be more at risk of having faulty professional judgment, which may negatively impact diagnosis, treatment planning, or may lead to client abuse (Kintzle, Yarvis, & Bride, 2013). There is a probability that mental-health workers will experience STS when they have been vicariously traumatized. Figley (1999) referred to STS as the normal set of emotions and behaviors that may follow new knowledge about a hurtful occurrence someone else has experienced. Secondary traumatic stress is the distress that comes as a result from aiding or the desire to help an anguished person; it is possible the distress can lead to STS disorder (Bride, 2007; Figley, 1995; Rzeszutek et al., 2015). Vicarious trauma and STS can affect a professional and the service they provide; therefore, studying ways in which organizations can provide support would benefit the worker, the client, and the organization.

Choi (2011) carried out a quantitative study to examine the relationships among features of STS of social workers who deliver treatment directly to victims of sexual assault or violence with a focus on support and work conditions. Choi (2011) did not mention the theoretical framework used for the study. The researcher employed a population sample consisting of 154 social workers who were recruited through the National Association of Social Workers (NASW). According to Choi (2011), social workers would probably come across victims of violence, including sexual assault, despite their area of work. Victims usually require many different services to deal with numerous issues after a traumatic incident. The research hypothesis was that social workers who received more organizational support and quality supervision would have a decreased incidence of STS and social workers who worked longer hours aiding victims would have increased levels of STS (Choi, 2011).

Data was collected using the STSS (Bride et al., 2004; Choi, 2011). The scale was used to measure symptoms of STS, which included intrusion, avoidance, and arousal. Agency support was studied with the use of the Social Structural Scale (SSS) which looks at four different aspects of social work. An individual survey was developed for this project, which included regularity of supervision, supervisor's attentiveness, supervisor's encouragement, and to what degree does the supervisor focus on the social workers professional and personal development (Choi, 2011). Demographics collected were age, years of (career) work, previous trauma, salary, gender, and ethnicity.

This research study had significant findings such as, managers who were more accessible, and planned strategically could prevent STS among the staff. The study was unsuccessful at confirming a substantial number of hours working with trauma was directly linked to STS, but did recognize the therapist's perception of the exposure was what determined STS (Choi, 2011). Another finding was STS is not directly an outcome of ineffective supervision; presence or absence of supervision was not linked to STS (Choi, 2011). The study found female social workers had more incidences of STS than male social workers. This could be related to factors such as empathy, previous trauma history, and more sensitivity (Choi, 2011). More importantly, the study indicates the more traumatic events the worker has experienced in his or her life, the more the worker is at jeopardy of STS. Eighty percent of the social workers in the study had undergone at least one traumatic event, and more than 70% of them had lived through either sexual assault or family violence (Choi, 2011). This study identified different factors that may contribute to STS; however, not one specific link was the single most determinant factor of STS. There may be an association between STS/VT and gender; it is too early to come to conclusions that female workers have higher chances of acquiring STS as opposed to male workers since there were less males in the current research study sample (Choi, 2011).

Connally (2012) conducted a quantitative study with 36 public mental-health workers at two sites in the San Francisco Bay, California (USA) area to examine the association among clinician STS and the clinician's gender, culture, and sexual orientation. According to Connally (2012), since earlier research studies indicated female providers were more at risk, researchers should contemplate demographic risk factors such as ethnicity, sexual orientation, and biological sex as the independent variables. The total research study's population sample of 36 included 17 males, 18 females, and one participant identifying as gender-queer. The research purpose was to study potential association between sex, ethnicity, sexual orientation, and levels of STS. Data was collected through the Professional Quality of Life (survey tool; Revision 3; ProQOL-CFS-III, 1995-2002).

The investigator found no connection between secondary trauma and the sex, sexual orientation, or ethnicity of the worker. The researcher did contemplate this could be due to the small sample size. The researcher also notes there was limited research on correlations to STS and clinician identity. Secondary traumatic stress and VT continue to be a phenomenon as the consequences can be negative as well as positive. Secondary traumatic stress and VT can be caused by exposure to traumatic accounts of client's experiences. Secondary traumatic stress can be experienced in different work settings, within different work roles, and affect the worker at different levels and has both emotional and psychological consequences.

Shannonhouse, Barden, Jones, Gonzales, and
Murphy (2016) conducted a study incorporating a
mixed-method approach to investigate the
experiences of 10 mental-health professionals.
Shannonhouse et al. (2016) carried out the research
using the community-grief scale with the mental-
health professionals that provided treatment to
fathers, mothers, and others responsible for the care
of the affected children, after a tragedy in the ABC
Day Care Center in Hermosillo, Mexico (2009). In the
disaster, 49 babies and young children were
murdered (by arson), and 93 others were seriously,
physically injured. Mixed-method designs are often
used to strengthen both quantitative and qualitative
models, providing a comprehensive examination into
the study (Shannonhouse et al., 2016). A
simultaneous triangulation approach was used to
comprehend the STS of the responding professional.
The authors did not mention the theoretical framework
behind the study.

The research study focused on the evaluation
and understanding of the reactions of MHP whom
served and also lived around or in the tragedy-
impacted area of Hermosillo, especially focusing on

the feelings and STS levels of the MHPs responding to the disaster. Semi-structured interviews were conducted and grounded on community data and STS literature. A quantitative component was carried out utilizing the ProQOL-5 and used to measure the consequences of aiding those who experience anguish and shock. The ProQOL-5 is a 30-entry measure with three scales, including compassion satisfaction, burnout, and STS. The ProQOL-5 was administered after the MHP concluded after four months of working with the parents, and then again after two months. Outcomes indicated that incidences of STS were reduced with the passage of time and a discussion of feelings associated with the experience. The workers providing direct services to the parents who experienced the death of a child displayed ongoing consequences of STS, even after the work was over (Shannonhouse et al., 2016). Mental-health professionals that worked with parents who suffered the death of a child or had a child who was badly hurt reported being psychologically affected months after the work ended. The researchers also indicated the need for a preparedness assessment and the integration of debriefing and support services when working with trauma survivors. Vicarious trauma and STS affect workers emotionally, psychologically, and physically. More qualitative studies should be conducted to explore workers feelings about future treatment options, as well as to look at organizations that employ the MHP workers and the support the MHPs have in place. Agency-based, mental-health workers, especially those involved in stressful cases, are in danger of STS. It is imperative that special attention is paid to the organizational characteristics that may affect workers who are exposed to STS (Caringi et al., 2017).

Caringi et al. (2017) conducted a study utilizing a mixed-method approach to exploring the incidence of STS, compassion fatigue, burnout, and compassion satisfaction among social workers in Montana. The researchers paid special attention to the organizational characteristics and peer support, and how it can possibly decrease the effect of the phenomena. The population was composed of 256 licensed social workers. The CSDT was used as the theoretical guide for the study. The researchers had three research questions. The first research question was related to social-workers' experience and how STS may be linked to the job, the second question examined social-workers' experience with STS and how do peers supporting each other affect and decrease the incidence of STS (Caringi et al. 2017). The STSS was utilized to study the degree of intrusion, avoidance and arousal symptoms connected with STS. The STSS verified indication of construct, discriminant, and factorial validity as well as increased levels of core consistency (Bride et al., 2004). The ProQOL, consisting of three subscales, was also used because it measured compassion, satisfaction, burnout, and STS. Unlike the STSS, the sub-scales in the ProQOL are measured independently. Demographic and job-related questions were used to gather data, which included current work duties, type of academic degrees (Caringi et al. 2017). Thirteen closed-ended and two open-ended questions were designed for this specific study to measure peer support. SPSS was used to analyze the surveys which included the STSS, the ProQOL, and the quantitative demographics. The qualitative component was analyzed using Atlas Ti.

The quantitative outcomes indicated workers in the study experienced substantial levels of STS, with 40.9% meeting the measures for PTSD according to the STSS (Caringi et al. 2017). ProQOL results indicated increased levels of burnout, compassion exhaustion, and STS. The qualitative data discovered themes linked with provider insights of influences that played a role in the incidence of STS (Caringi et al. 2017). These studies continue to demonstrate the effects of VT/STS on the helping professional (Caringi et al., 2017; Connally, 2012; Shannonhouse et al., 2016) but the studies fail to identify and provide treatment. Studies have repeatedly demonstrated how VT and STS affect the working professionals who work with trauma (Caringi et al., 2017; Choi, 2011; Connally, 2012; Shannonhouse et al., 2016).

VT and STS are noteworthy occupational hazards for mental-health professionals, possibly carrying undesirable repercussion on the private relationship(s) of the worker (Branson et al., 2014). Mental-health professionals would benefit from ongoing training, peer support, ongoing supervision, and organizational support. Although these propositions are not without value, they fail to identify the intellectual strategies required to aid mental-health workers in dealing with worker's ongoing vulnerability to client anguish (Cox & Steiner, 2013). Research outcomes demonstrate that VT and STS can affect individuals regardless of age or gender, job title or work environment. If there is interaction with traumatized clients, there will be a risk of VT and STS. While researchers continue rigorous studies on the phenomenon, it would benefit mental health providers to practice self-care in addition to the other supports. Best practices in physical health and mental-health care begin with self-care (Goodwin & Richards, 2017).

Self-Care

Self-care is defined as an intricate, complex process of meaningful engagement of strategies directed at overall well-being (Dorociak et al., 2017b). These strategies encourage individuals to adapt healthy ways (of living, both physically and mentally), through actions such as searching for their own private therapy, dedicating time to their personal relationships, making changes to the routine work schedule, and participating in out of work activities (Dorociak et al., 2017b).

Although self-care is presently being encouraged in the field, its importance and definition has not been fully studied in the field of mental health (Cox & Steiner, 2013). Researchers identified self-care as an ethical need for professionals (Norcross & Guy, 2007) to incorporate self-care practices that fit into overall categories of everyday living or the workplace environment (Cox & Steiner, 2013). Recommendations are that workers eat nutritious meals, exercise, and participate in recreational and spiritual activities as self-care practices (Cox & Steiner, 2013). While engaged at work, workers have been encouraged to take breaks while at work, stabilize caseloads, and seek support from co-workers (Cox & Steiner, 2013; Pryce et al., 2007; Saakvitne & Pearlman, 1996). While these suggestions are all well-intentioned, the needs of therapists may increase and change as they develop their career as providers.

The mental-health profession holds high regard to service provision. Service provision is instilled in every worker that their clients are the priority. As mentioned in the profession's code of ethics, the social workers main objective is to aid individuals in need, target social issues, and help all individuals beyond self-interest (NASW, 2017; Wheeler & McClain, 2015). NASW makes clear that social workers are obliged to sustain a rock-hard pledge to the people they serve and their managers; it specifically points out a duty to guarantee the consumer's (client's) well-being is prioritized and services are not disrupted without reasonable cause (Cox & Steiner, 2013; NASW, 2017). What is not stated is devotion to these obligations necessitates employees need to also practice appropriate self-care (Cox & Steiner, 2013). There have been studies that explore well-being and self-care, however, none of these studies defined a specific strategy. "Learning to pay attention to and be respectful of one's needs and to meet them responsibly, is a lifelong task for the therapist as well as for our patients" (Baker, 2003a, p. 60).

Shannon, Simmelink-McCleary, Im, Becher, and Crook-Lynn (2014) employed a qualitative method to examine self-care strategies of 17 learners in a trauma-related class. Data was gathered using

the student journals which were submitted four times
during the course. The researchers wanted to study
the progress of self-care strategies among social work
graduate students using Consensual Qualitative
Research (CQR). Outcomes demonstrated the
participants profited from self-care practices
introduced during this time. The study also suggested
the students did struggle with developing self-care
practices. The authors stated comprehension of how
the participants became introduced into the practice
of practical self-care may have contributed
substantially to the deterrence of VT and exhaustion
among the participants exposed to difficult situations
in their work (Shannon et al., 2014).

Beaumont, Durkin, Hollins-Martin, and Carson
(2016) carried out a quantitative investigation to
measure associations related to self-empathy, fatigue,
well-being, and exhaustion in cognitive behavioral
therapy students. The mixed sample consisted of
counseling and psychotherapy students. Quantitative
validated surveys were used for data collection. The
surveys included Professional Quality of Life Scale,
the Self-Compassion Scale, Short Warwick, and the
Edinburg Mental Well-being Scale (Beaumont et al.,

2016). These surveys measured associations among self-empathy, fatigue, well-being, and exhaustion (Beaumont et al., 2016). The authors did not mention a theoretical framework for this study. The authors found fatigue and exhaustion exist in the field of healthcare and the practice of self-empathy could help practitioners manage symptoms and improve their professional quality of life. The authors also suggested that self-care practices may decrease symptoms of fatigue, self-criticism, and exhaustion while increasing a sense of overall wellness (Beaumont et al., 2016). This was one example of an attempt to explore suggestions for self-care in the professional field.

Research demonstrates there is necessity for self-care, however, there are only a few studies that demonstrate how this is accomplished This has been a concern for years, as several authors have suggested there are influences impacting practitioners in ways that make consideration to self-care and continued-wellness practices crucial to conduct effective treatment (Baker, 2003a; Barnett, Baker, Elman, & Schoener, 2007; Dattilio, 2015; Goodwin & Richards, 2017; Wise, Hersh, & Gibson, 2012).

Review of Research Literature and
Methodological Literature Specific
to the Topic or Research Question

As a profession, social workers tend to
disregard the significance of creating a justifiable
equilibrium related to caring for clients and caring for
themselves, (Wise et al., 2012). Social workers fail to
address their own mental-health and health needs,
therefore, potentially affecting the treatment they
provide for their clients. Wise et al. (2012) shares a
2000 year-old quote from Rabbi Hillel the Elder who
stated; "If I am not for myself, who will be for me." (p.
487).

Overview of Mental Health Workers

Mental-health workers (e.g., social workers)
are employed in-one of the most demanding fields
with psychologically difficult situations in which it is
anticipated they are able to serve people who are
anguished due to complicated and chronic illnesses
found within the gamut of mental distress (Dattilio,

2015). This raises the concern of why mental-health workers would not find it in their best interest to seek help for themselves when needed (Dattilio, 2015). Although these workers experience similar work-related stressors to other human-service employees, the inherent features of working in the field of mental health incorporates additional pressure (Cetrano et al., 2017). Serious risk factors are seen to be chiefly relevant to care within the field. One recognized factor is the association that workers experience with individuals (clients) undergoing or have experienced suffering (Cetrano et al., 2017). Through exposure of client's revelations and sharing of traumatic experiences, mental-health workers, and others in the helping professions are at risk of a number of different symptoms (Cetrano et al., 2017). Indicators of these symptoms may include sadness, uneasiness, intrusive thoughts, evasion, and intellectual shifts, as well as work-related and personal issues (Cetrano et al., 2017). Because of the sharing of traumatic experiences, mental-health workers are subject to vicarious traumatization and/or STS, and the workers personal and professional lives can be affected by their work (Tavormina & Clossy, 2015). Even though most mental-health workers employed in clinical settings provide treatment to trauma victims, some were not properly trained (Cook, Simiola, Ellis, & Thompson, 2017). Prevention of these negative effects of working with trauma victims requires education, oversight, and discussion associated with treatment for this type of work (Cook et al., 2017). Mental-health professionals should identify self-care strategies in addition to obtaining trauma training. The significance of self-care in mental-health workers has been identified, however, there is not enough information already clearly identified that can assist the workers in the field of mental health (e.g., social workers) manage stress when faced with individuals who have suffered or have experienced trauma (Cox & Steiner, 2013).

Vicarious Trauma History

Vicarious trauma is well-defined as changes in 'the self' that a worker undergoes from vicarious interaction with distressed individuals and the encounters of their experiences: its trademark is disturbance in their faith, or a disturbance in the workers apparent sense of optimism (Shively, 2017). In the 1990's, the concepts related to therapist trauma was broadly investigated (Figley, 1995; McCann & Pearlman, 1990b). Two terms frequently used to intellectualize worker trauma as a consequence of working with anguished individuals were VT and STS disorder (Bell & Robinson, 2013). If the mental-health worker is not prepared to listen to their patients and articulate their patient's detached or partially remembered experiences, they may, in turn, dissociate the experiences themselves leaving them vulnerable and open to unexpected intrusive, and often unexplained reactions, not only in the professional sector, but in their everyday lives (Boulanger, 2016).

The effects do not arise solely from one therapeutic association, known to occur over time, with cumulative therapeutic interactions (Pearlman & Maclan, 1995). Although studies have often focused on the effect of direct experience of trauma … mental-health workers are vicariously exposed to traumatic experiences through their work (Brockhouse, Msetfi, Cohen, & Joseph, 2011; Pearlman & Saakvitne, 1995). Other factors that may influence vicarious traumatization in the worker is their own history of trauma, significance of traumatic life issues, spiritual style, personal style, intellectual growth, existing stressors, and support system (Pearlman & Maclan, 1995).

Vicarious trauma has been an issue for years and often leads to physical and psychological difficulties (Dombo & Gray, 2013). Over time, VT continues to be a concern when addressing mental-health workers and how the phenomenon affects the worker's daily professional and personal lives. Assets that make workers most successful with their clients, such as sympathy, kindness, and consideration, can also leave them at risk of undesirable and damaging outcomes (Thompson, Amatea, & Thompson, 2014). Trauma can be as devastating for the mental-health worker as it is for the individual sharing the information.

Mental Health Workers, Vicarious Trauma, and Self-Care

Strategies for self-care adapted by mental-health workers can be utilized during the therapeutic interaction, therefore, promoting healthy relationships and positive outcomes. According to Bell and Robinson (2013), the rewards of self-care – such as the capability of being present, client encouragement, and a boosted therapeutic relationship – will reflect within the treatment session, providing not only healing for the counselor, but also modeling for the client. When a worker experiences VT, they may distance themselves from the therapeutic relationship. Vicarious trauma can hinder the worker's capability to be present in the moment or to provide treatment (Boulanger, 2016). In addition to self-care, workers should be encouraged to engage in ongoing training regarding VT and how it affects them and the treatment they provide. Aparicio, Michalopoulos, and Unick (2013) noted the more professional experience and increased support mental-health workers receive, the less likelihood there is of experiencing VT. Proficient self-care can be expressed as the application of services and strategies by mental-health workers (e.g., social workers) to preserve their individual, emotional, and spiritual needs while fulfilling their work-related responsibilities (Figley, 1995; NASW, 2017; Newell & Nelson-Gardell, 2014).

The clinical-learning setting and culture of the professionals in the field of social work is saturated with implications and obvious messages regarding self-sufficiency, competition, perfectionism, being a workaholic, and avoiding displays of fragility or weakness (Runyan, 2017). Social-work course-curriculum syllabi are not comprised of, nor offer, specific skills social workers can use to incorporate into their career preparation when dealing with empathy or compassion – without decomposing from VT (Runyan, 2017). The well-being of the mental-health worker needs to become an essential quality (Runyan, 2017). Mental-health workers would rather dismiss the notion of looking for services due to fear or embarrassment and loss of confidentiality (Dattilio, 2015). Studies demonstrate service provision is affected when the worker has become affected by either VT or STS (Dorociak et al, 2017; Knight, 2013; Sansbury et al., 2015). Who is responsible for mental-health workers' self-care? The individual, the employer organization, or the governing boards? According to Packenham (2015), self-care is principally an individual's responsibility; however professional organizations, psychology accreditation bodies, and licensing boards should have a part in the accountability – even having a duty in promoting self-care within the profession.

Cox and Steiner (2013) conducted a participatory research study to explore the prevalence of vicarious traumatic stress in the social-work field and strategies used to overcome or prevent VT. The researchers used the CSDT as a framework for their study. The study sample consisted of six diverse public and private social service establishments in California. All participants (n = 48) were actively providing services to traumatized individuals while the study was conducted. The participants were in different roles in social services and work experience ranged from one year to 40 years of experience. Social workers who consented to participate in the study were asked to complete the Trauma and Attachment Belief Scale (TABS; Pearlman & Maclan 1995). The scale measured for beliefs, assumptions, and expectations. The participants then participated in focus groups of six to 11 per group, where they were asked to describe encounters experienced with client trauma or suffering and their thoughts and reactions associated with the experiences.

Participants were then asked to share the support tools they used in dealing with these experiences.

The TABS results indicated therapists who had a personal-trauma history presented higher scores than other clinicians, female clinicians had a reduced score in spiritual well-being, and there was a significant correlation between an emergence of PTSD in trauma therapists and TABS scores. The qualitative-analysis focus groups demonstrated an array of traumatic situations which affected workers. Child-welfare workers described incidents of trauma after they were shown photographs as evidence. Mental-health workers shared experiences associated with the presence of patients screaming and moaning in mental-health hospitals. Domestic-violence workers shared experiences of abused and tortured clients.

The findings demonstrated thinking patterns and themes associated with strengths and abilities in social workers when managing with a client's pain, suffering, and trauma. The researchers suggested social workers with a history of trauma should seek additional help, supervision should be available to trauma workers, and organizations should provide a culture of care that enables workers to process these experiences (Cox & Steiner, 2013).

Kulkarni, Bell, Hartman, and Herman-Smith (2013) conducted a quantitative-research study to explore organizational factors that contribute to worker wellness, avoiding negative effects, and supporting positive results for practitioners. The participants (n = 236) were practitioners employed in agencies that serve victims of domestic violence in the Southwest region of the United States. The participants filled out a Web-based survey targeting perception of workplace factors (e.g., caseloads, community, impartiality, and workplace values) (Kulkarni et al., 2013). The researchers theorized associations among workers and their work settings could indicate compassion satisfaction. Findings indicated there were organizational mismatches significant in risks associated with burnout and STS. These mismatches included unmanageable caseloads which led to burnout. Findings indicated STS is associated with the worker's state of mind when they have no say in the workload (Kulkarni et al., 2013). The researchers indicate job fulfillment is associated with a longer work history in the field of domestic violence and with workers who share the standards of their work setting (Kulkarni et al., 2013). Researchers indicated organizations that promote wellness and protect workers will benefit from a healthy workforce (Kulkarni et al., 2013).

Wagaman, Geiger, Shockley, and Seigal (2015) conducted a quantitative study employing (n = 173) social workers to investigate the association between empathy, exhaustion, STS, and compassion satisfaction utilizing the Empathy Assessment Index and the Professional Quality of Life instruments. The researchers assumed increased measures of empathy could be a correlation to decreased measures of burnout and STS, as well as higher measures of compassion fulfillment (Wagaman et al., 2015). The outcomes suggested there are elements of empathy that can avert or reduce burnout and STS, at the same time increasing compassion satisfaction, and empathy should be merged with teachings during the social worker's professional life (Wagaman et al., 2015). Mental-health workers change professionally over their careers indicating a potential developmental component to the needs of the worker – both professionally and personally (Dorociak et al., 2017).

Dorociak et al. (2017) conducted a study using archived data from two previously-conducted surveys to examine early-career, mid-career, and later-career mental-health workers with three queries. The questions dealt with personal and professional wellness, work-connected stresses and resources, and using those self-care strategies across career phases (Dorociak et al., 2017). The outcomes indicated professional-wellness changes over the worker's career span with a greater emphasis on overall wellness as the practitioner evolves. Outcomes also indicated – early in the profession – there are superior worker-related demands with fewer resources (Dorociak et al., 2017) as MHP workers (in later stages of their career) may engage in more self-care than those in their earlier careers. Dorociak et al. (2017) states "an emphasis on developing and encouraging self-care strategies should begin as early as possible to foster a culture of self-care that continues throughout the professional lifespan" (p. 436).

Santana and Fouad (2017) conducted a study to develop and validate a Self-Care Behavioral Inventory. The researchers divided the project into two separate studies. The two studies were established in an attempt of developing an instrument that would quantify self-care strategies practiced by doctoral students. The first study employed a sample of (n = 28) doctoral students to produce an entry selection grounded on the Self-Care Assessment Worksheet. The second study (n = 111) of a population of doctoral students examined the psychometric properties of the updated inventory (Santana & Fouad, 2017). The authors tested three hypotheses. Hypothesis one indicated a noteworthy association between self-care, overall perception of capability, and wellness, and that learners with increased scores of self-care would have favorable competency and wellness numbers (Santana & Fouad, 2017). Hypothesis two predicted an association between self-care and burnout, demonstrated by increased measures in self-care would have decreased measures in the burnout portion (Santana & Fouad, 2017). Hypothesis three indicated an association among learner educational practices and occurrence of self-care, indicating interns would have higher scores as opposed to practice students (Santana & Fouad, 2017). The findings suggested – as trainees advance in professional levels – the incidence of self-care does not change, which can be an indicator of autonomy as practice progresses (Santana & Fouad, 2017).

The researchers discussed that learners comprehended the significance of self-care, and when to initiate it when treating individuals (Santana & Fouad, 2017). While there has been more quantitative and mixed methods research conducted at exploring the phenomenon regarding VT and STS, there has been little qualitative research at addressing the self-care needs of mental-health professionals in this area. Qualitative studies would be geared toward exploring lived experiences through narrative accounts of the worker story.

Phenomenology

Phenomenology is an approach utilized in investigating an individual's interpretations of beliefs and their understandings of the world (Ellis, 2016). Edmund Husserl (1858-1938) is accredited as being the founder of phenomenology (Ellis, 2016). Phenomenology is a method of analysis that pursues to comprehend understanding (Moustakas, 1994) that investigates the phenomena and how it is understood and lived by individuals (Lester, 1999, Sheehan, 2014). In phenomenology, the researcher uses purposeful sampling, as purposeful sampling selects individuals who have experienced the phenomenon being investigated (Ellis, 2016). Qualitative studies require fewer participants than quantitative research studies. Random participants would not benefit the research from the phenomenology viewpoint because a researcher cannot assume this individual has experienced the phenomenon being investigated. Participants would be expected to produce genuine, solid, and intensive material related to the research theory or study question to permit the researcher to deliver a substantial explanation of the phenomenon (Cleary, Horsfall, & Hayter, 2014). The type and number of participants will depend on the knowledge desired, the purpose, any potential benefits, and validity of the study (Cleary et al., 2014). The subjects can potentially answer the research questions from their lived experiences. Different literature reviews recommend various sample sizes, but between six and 20 participants would suffice

(Ellis, 2016). Lower numbers of sample populations targeted for a qualitative research study are appropriate due to the specific concentration of the interview questions. Four selection principles for sample choices in phenomenology are: (a) small numbers allow for intense investigations, (b) individuals are chosen purposefully (to answer a topic-specific research question), (c) it is more commonly sequential instead of predetermined (d) and there is a rationale for selection, with the potential for participants to have specific 'experience' with the research theory or topic questions (Ellis, 2016). The researcher looks for patterns, themes, and sub-themes generated by the narratives to answer the research questions. The transcendental-phenomenological approach is used in this research study as it will incorporate the lived experience of mental-health workers with VT. Transcendental phenomenology (TPh), adds magnitudes to studies of experience using qualitative studies (Sheehan, 2014). Moustakas (1994) depicts the core process that simplifies the origin of knowledge as the epoche, Transcendental-Phenomenological Reduction, and Imaginative Variation. Transcendental

phenomenology is grounded in the notion of
separating all predetermined thoughts (epoche) to
clearly see the phenomena using untainted lenses,
therefore permitting the correct understanding of the
phenomena (Moustakas, 1994; Sheehan, 2014).
Moustakas (1994) claims phenomenology as the most
suitable approach regarding the discovery of
unfolding collective experiences associated to
phenomena.

Petrovich and Cronley (2015) conducted a
qualitative research study utilizing the
phenomenological approach to delve into the lived
experience of desolate homelessness in Fort Worth,
Texas. Eighteen participants were part of the
investigation, 13 were permanent inhabitants, and five
were 'passing through' the geographic area (Petrovich
& Cronley, 2015). Quantifiable approaches were
utilized to gather demographics such as age, gender,
race, and the vagrancy history of the individuals
(Petrovich & Cronley, 2015). The authors provided
participants with a gift card for their time. Interviews
were recorded and conducted in natural settings to
gather the data. The researchers also took field
notes. The interviews lasted approximately two

hours. The settings were areas in the community such as on the street or beneath a bridge where the study participants gathered, felt safe, and were comfortable. The semi-structured questions were designed to explore the participant's path to homelessness, their lived experience of their current conditions, and why the situation continued (Petrovich & Cronley, 2015). The interview questions were related to the path to homelessness, participant's feelings related to living 'the street life,' and feelings around seeking services from a shelter (Petrovich & Cronley, 2015). Results showed participants succumbed to homelessness for different reasons, but the most prevalent reasons for the homelessness were loss and social segregation (Petrovich & Cronley, 2015). The phenomenological approach is utilized in research studies to gather rich 'lived' information from the viewpoints of the people who experience the phenomenon (Petrovich & Cronley, 2015).

Day et al. (2017) conducted a qualitative research study utilizing a phenomenological approach to provide descriptions of the collective perceptions of eight mental-health workers who helped those who

experienced the shooting catastrophe at Virginia Tech
(2007). Day et al. collected data and explored
collective trauma, VT, compassion fatigue, vicarious
resilience, and post-traumatic growth (Day et al.,
2017). The purpose of Day et al.'s research study
was to comprehend the phenomenon from the
viewpoint of the clinician and the connotation they
allocated to the event. The phenomenon in this study
was shared trauma, or a joint-traumatic realism, which
refers to occurrences in which the clinician and client
experience the trauma concurrently (Day et al., 2017).
The researchers used the constructivist theory as a
theoretical framework. The research questions in the
study captured the lived experiences of the mental-
health workers who responded to the shootings,
regarding the phenomenon of shared trauma with the
people they served, in addition to what were the
meanings, structures, and essences of these
experiences of shared trauma (Day et al., 2017). The
findings suggested that, in times of traumatic disaster,
workers look for guidance, supportive leadership, and
their own private counseling so their negative
experiences do not prevent them from working
positively or effectively (Day et al., 2017). Mental-

health workers, managers, and supervisors would mentally and emotionally benefit from additional training in the area of effective treatment and work place involvement in the event of catastrophes (Day et al., 2017).

Synthesis of the Research Findings

Vicarious trauma is well defined as a change in 'the self' that a mental health, social worker, or first responder may undergo due to vicarious interaction with distressed victims and the shared experience of their trauma. Vicarious trauma's trademark is a disturbance in spiritual beliefs or a disturbance in the trauma worker's apparent understanding of optimism (Shively, 2017). There are studies demonstrating the personal and professional damage VT and STS can cause mental-health workers. Studies suggest service provisions are affected when the worker has become affected by either VT or STS (Dorociak et al., 2017; Knight, 2013; Sansbury et al., 2015). Vicarious trauma and STS can cause disruptions in other areas of the worker's life. Branson et al. (2014) concluded higher levels of VT/STS cause a lowered level of sex

drive. This would affect a worker on a personal level.
Finklestein et al. (2015) concluded the mental-health
worker could be affected – not only by the work with
the traumatized client – but also by the geographic or
environmental area where the work takes place. His
study took place in Gaza where workers were also
experienced primary trauma due to exposure to
rocket bombardments and explosions. Middleton and
Potter (2015) concluded, in their study with child-
welfare workers, that VT impacted staff turnover with
workers leaving the career position earlier due to their
exposure to VT/STS. Not everyone will be affected
by VT/STS. Some studies show VT may lead to
potential growth. Hernandez-Wolfe et al. (2015) and
McCormack and Adams (2016) concluded that
vicarious resilience may coexist with VT; special
attention should be paid to worker supervision, which
would decrease the chances of employees
experiencing VT. According to Hyatt-Burkhart (2014),
practitioners can demonstrate positive indicators (e.g.,
gratitude for living; a determination to live a better
quality of life) from their experience, similar to
individuals who were directly impacted by the event.
While some mental-health workers are affected

negatively, others are affected in positive ways. Soon after a traumatic event, individuals will undergo a period of evolution and constructive changes (Hyatt-Burkhart, 2014).

Halevi and Idisis (2017) concluded in their study that workers with their own history of trauma may be more at risk for VT and STS ... a theory supported by Pearlman and Maclan's research (1995). Vicarious trauma suggests deviations in the worker's continued ways of experiencing self, others, and the world may have detrimental effects on service provision and personal lives (Edelkott et al., 2016; Pearlman & Maclan, 1995; Shively, 2017).

This literature review indicated that VT and STS may cause damage in the mental-health workers professional and personal lives, but also cause professional growth (Hernandez-Wolfe et al., 2015). Even under these conditions, workers should be provided with effective supervision and positive support (Hernandez-Wolfe et al., 2015).

The query for self-care also demonstrates an understanding of the need for self-care for professionals. There are no identified studies concluding specific steps to ameliorate this issue.

Self-care can be expressed as the application of
services and approaches by mental-health workers
(e.g., social workers) that can aid in the preservation
of their personal, emotional and spiritual needs while
providing valuable services (Figley, 1999; NASW,
2017; Newell & Nelson-Gardell, 2014).

There are no identified studies directly linking
mental-health workers (e.g., social workers) to
personal and professional self-care. Although self-
care has been promoted in the work setting, there is
no clear understanding of self-care practices or
research explorations in the field of mental health
(Cox & Steiner, 2013). Researchers recognized self-
care is an ethical imperative for professionals
(Norcross & Guy, 2007) to incorporate those self-care
strategies that fit into universal clusters in everyday
life or workplace modifications (Cox & Steiner, 2013).
Research suggests a need for self-care, but there are
few studies that demonstrate how this is conducted.
Researchers have suggested there are issues that
impact working professionals in ways that make
consideration of self-care and ongoing wellness
crucial for service provision (Baker, 2003a; Barnett et
al., 2007; Dattilio, 2015; Goodwin & Richard, 2017;

Wise et al., 2012). Baker et al.'s studies were geared towards agency support and the need for a culture of care within the organizations (Cox & Steiner, 2013; Kulkarni et al., 2013). Researchers indicate organizations promoting wellness and protection of workers benefit from a healthy workforce (Kulkarni et al., 2013).

While there is also a belief that workers change and evolve over time during their professional careers, their needs change as well (Dorociak et al., 2017; Wagaman et al., 2015). Younger workers may need additional support; older workers may have learned how to deal with work demands. This turns attention to mental-health workers, VT, and self-care … a connecting link to add to the body of knowledge.

According to Dorociak et al. (2017), when workers are healthy, outcomes are positive. There are preliminary studies which indicate self-care is linked to professional well-being and positive results (Dorociak et al., 2017). The social-work profession respects service provision, and social workers are instructed to care for clients first – as mentioned in the code of ethics (principal objective is to primarily aid individuals and provide service to others; NASW,

2017; Wheeler & McClain, 2015). Special attention should be directed towards service providers since they are the individuals at the forefront of client care. Beyond deterrence of professional and personal issues, practical and continuous self-care improves everyday quality of life and wellness, consequently contributing to the ideal career performance (Zahniser et al., 2017).

Without proper professional attention, social workers are left vulnerable to the shared burden of VT or STS (Molnar et al., 2017). Professionals having suffered trauma and a personal history of trauma may remain silent behind an emotional screen of denial and professionalism (Molnar et al., 2017). If not addressed, these professionals may suffer further VT/ STS damage, resulting in job loss, career resignation, or burnout. It would be beneficial to the organizations that employ these types of mental health, social worker, and/or first responders, as well as individuals that educate them, and public policymakers, to address these related issues. This research study may result in increased job retention and decrease turnover.

Critique of Previous Research

While VT will not be experienced by all mental-health workers and VT or STS may not impact these workers negatively, those that are affected would benefit from healthy working conditions. Self-care and a philosophy of self-care within the work environment would improve client-service provision and improve worker wellness. Mental-health professionals are exposed to VT daily in their everyday work experience (Molnar et al., 2017).

There has been an awareness on the significance of self-care for workers within the field of mental health (Dorociak et al., 2017). Mental-health professionals encounter stressors they must address to function in the work setting and their personal lives. This stress, if not addressed, may have negative consequences for their clients' service provision (Molnar et al., 2017). Work-related difficulties can become hazardous when delivering services to disturbed and violence exposed individuals and can be a threat to workforce equilibrium (Molnar et al., 2017). The progression of vicarious trauma can result in undesirable results compared to a downward spiral which begins when stress cannot be managed leads to mental and emotional, anguish (Dorociak et al., 2017).

Stress, lack of self-care, and the absence of a 'culture of care' within a working organization can be detrimental to the helping and social work professions. A coordinated response from researchers, politicians, and organizational leaders will help professionals who have been left susceptible to the burden of trauma accumulated from chronic and acute distress also known as VT and STS (Molnar et al., 2017).

This literature review was conducted to explore previous studies on VT/STS, self-care, and the mental health worker. Although there are studies exploring the phenomenon separately and suggest further studies on self-care especially in relation to mental-health professionals, no study addresses the mental health worker, VT, and self-care. There are fewer qualitative studies related to VT/STS and self-care. The research primarily addresses VT, STS or self-care in relation to specific topics, such as staff turnover (Middleton & Potter, 2015), personal consequences such as sex drive (Branson et al.,

2014), or shared trauma (Halevi & Idisis, 2017). Regarding self-care, there are suggestions for an improved culture of care within organizations as in studies conducted by Cox and Steiner (2013) and Kulkarni et al. (2013). Little research addresses the issue of self-care regarding practice or suggested strategies.

Santana and Fouad (2017) conducted a study to develop and validate a Self-Care Behavioral Inventory. A self-care inventory would be useful in identifying the use of self-care. The STSS (Bride, 2007) measures for STS. There are other scales that measure quality of life. There are measures to identify VT, STS, and self-care; however, there is no indication of a valid measuring instrument how self-care is practiced by mental-health workers.

While there has been more quantitative and mixed methods research conducted at exploring the phenomenon regarding VT and STS, there has been little qualitative research at addressing the self-care needs of mental-health professionals. Qualitative studies would be geared toward exploring lived experiences through narrative accounts of the worker story. It would be beneficial to educators, policymakers, and organizations if research could demonstrate accounts of lived experiences of mental-health workers who are dealing with VT or STS. In looking at accounts of lived experiences, attention could be placed at the need for self-care practices, as they should not be the sole responsibility of the mental-health worker.

Chapter 3

Methodology

Purpose of the Study

The purpose of this qualitative study was to investigate mental-health workers' lived experiences of coping with VT, and how they incorporate self-care in a community mental-health clinic in a northeastern state. Self-care strategies may be described as looking for therapy, spending time with loved ones, scheduling changes in daily lives, and being involved in organizational events (Dorociak et al., 2017). Molnar et al. (2017) concluded practitioners (e.g., social workers) face demands – both personal and work-related – that can affect service provision. Molnar et al. (2017) explained these demands cause increased stress, that – if left unattended – may have negative consequences on the worker, both professionally and personally. Occupational hazards may occur while delivering services to traumatized and violence exposed individuals. By investigating the effects of VT on the overall helping experience, professionals in the mental-health field would be better equipped to manage their own daily experiences, which may cause internal turmoil or feelings of inadequacy.

Research Design

Qualitative research is an organized method of gathering data through the collection of interviews, and other non-numerical data processes; it has specific outcomes that unearths knowledge while allowing participants to share their lived experiences (Swanson & Holton, 2005). In this action-research study, transcendental phenomenology was used to examine the connection between mental-health workers, how they cope when working with VT, and how they practice self-care.

The transcendental-phenomenology approach involves a revisit to detailed accounts of the experience that provides a basis for thoughtful structural analysis that represents the spirit of the moment (Moustakas, 1994). Vicarious trauma – also known as secondary traumatic stress – is a phenomenon experienced by helping professionals due to hearing stories or accounts of harmful experiences shared by their patients. Since the intention of this research study was to investigate the lived experiences of mental-health workers and how they cope with VT, the phenomenology methodology was the more beneficial approach.

The core steps in the transcendental analytical path are epoche, transcendental-phenomenological reduction, and imaginative variation (Moustakas, 1994). Using the total transcript of each participant's interview, a search was conducted for emerging patterns and themes. The preliminary findings of these repeated patterns and themes were followed by reduction and elimination. The reduction and elimination were determined by whether the expression contained a moment of experience and whether that moment was sufficiently understood. The repeated expressions were identified as codes or nodes as expressed in NVivo 12 software, which was used to manage and organize the data. NVivo 12 data-coding software explores data to uncover the developing themes, patterns, and phrases using word queries for analysis (QSR International, 2016).

Transcendental phenomenology (TPh) brings added magnitudes to studies of human experience through qualitative studies (Sheehan, 2014). Transcendental phenomenology is built on the notion that once preconceived ideas (epoche) are set aside the phenomena can be seen clearly; thus, permitting the correct gist of the phenomena to arise with and within their own meaning (Moustakas, 1994; Sheehan, 2014). Moustakas (1994) posited phenomenology as an appropriate instrument for discovering and unfolding shared experiences related to the phenomena.

Epoche is when all pre-judgments are set aside, and the interview opens with an unbiased and receptive presence (Moustakas, 1994). The second-core process is transcendental-phenomenological reduction, which refers to: (a) bracketing, which is giving the phenomenon the entire attention and focus of the study; (b) horizonalization, which is giving equal value to statements, delimited horizons, or meanings; (c) invariant qualities and themes which is clustering nonrepetitive constituents to make themes; (d) personal textural accounts, which is an expressive integration of the themes of each participant; and (e) complex textural accounts, which is an mixing of all accounts into a universal descriptions (Moustakas, 1994). The third-core process, imaginative variation, refers to looking for possible meanings using imagination, different frames of reference, and a variety of perspectives (Moustakas, 1994).

Data was gathered, analyzed, and triangulated using the STSS, a short demographic survey, in-depth interviews, post-interview member checking, and a researcher's reflective journal. Triangulation refers to the combining of multiple sources of data collected to confirm the findings. Data collection included the participant's demographics, gender, age, length of time working at the current agency, and length of years working in the mental-health field. The STSS was used to identify secondary traumatic symptoms in helping professionals. Participants who scored a 28 and above on the total score were considered to have VT. Patterns and themes were identified and established through collective lived experiences described by the subjects. Interviews were conducted in a safe space and then later transcribed. A field journal was created to document and establish an audit trail in addition to data collection. The interviews took place in a confidential and safe place. Post-interview member checking was conducted by sending the participants a summary of the transcription to allow them to check for accuracy. Member checking (informant feedback) was conducted to aid with validity, credibility, and transferability. A journal was kept in which observations, reflections, and other issues that arose during the research process were documented.

Target Population and Participant Selection

The population for this study consisted of mental-health workers employed in a community mental-health clinic in a northeastern state. The site selected for the research was a mental-health clinic which is part of a nonprofit, community-based organization offering mental health services and programs to traumatized individuals for over 30 years. The sample for the study consisted of 12 participants currently working in the mental-health field in different capacities. Inclusion criteria included: (a) any prospective participant employed as a mental health worker, either by licensure or job description, including LPCs, LMSWs, LCSWs, social workers, family coordinators, and intake workers; (b) a total score of 28 or above on the STSS; (c) being over the age of 18 years; and (d) living in the geographic area. The target population sample included both male and female. Exclusion criteria included anyone with an active *DSM* (5th ed.) diagnosis, students, volunteers at the research home, or scoring below a 28 on the STSS.

Information about the study was provided to prospective participants during a staff meeting. Sample selection criteria were shared and all questions about the research were addressed. Interested prospective participants then scheduled a meeting so additional questions could be answered. Prospective participants were then asked if they wanted to be part of the study. A group of prospective participants interested in the study moved to a private room where the researcher described the study again and answered clarifying questions. Prospective participants who fit the selection criteria signed a consent form and were administered the

STSS that day. If a prospective participant did not agree to go further, they were thanked for their time and released from the study. Scores from the STSS were presented to respective participants. Out of 12 prospective participants, two scored under a 28 on the STSS. The process of sample selection continued until a full sample size (N = 12) was achieved.

This research involved VT, also known as STS. This secondary trauma is experienced by helping professionals due to hearing stories or accounts of harmful experiences shared by their patient / clients. Due to the topic and the trauma involved, the participants were identified as being at possible risk for mental-health issues. All ethical considerations and precautions were taken to ensure participant safety. Resources were provided to participants; debriefing and counseling were made available. Steps were taken to ensure confidentiality and safekeeping of participants notes and records. A confidentiality agreement was signed to ensure data from interviews remained confidential. Psychological harm was mitigated by providing additional resources for counseling and or employee assistant programs if participants in the research study felt they needed the assistance. Adequate informed consent allowed participants to decide if they wanted to be part of the study, guided by clear and accurate information.

Procedures

Nonprofit-community organizations, that offered mental-health services, were contacted to obtain a research location. The literature review on VT and lack of self-care was presented to establish the need for the study. For purposes of the investigation, a site was selected based on the mental-health workers employed and the services offered. According to Hacker (2013), to learn more about the researchers, their goals, their background, and their expectations for partnership, a face-to-face meeting is recommended.

After an agreement was established between the research site and the researcher, a meeting was scheduled to present the study to the mental-health workers. Site approval was obtained to comply with Capella University ethics and professional mandates, Institutional Review Board research ethics requirements, and the Chief Executive Officer of the clinic.

A staff meeting was organized in which the research study was presented to the prospective participants and qualifying information was shared. Participants were informed their priorities and perspectives would be considered, respected, and valued in the research agenda and processes followed (Hacker, 2013). Interested prospective participants were informed they could contact the researcher to clarify and ask questions or schedule a time to meet and have the STSS administered. The researcher left flyers with contact information. Prospective participants were also allowed the opportunity to take the STSS at their own convenience. Qualifying, interested, prospective participants were directed towards the next steps in the research study, which included signing the informed consent, the administration of the STSS, and scheduling the interview. Prospective participants who did not qualify or did not score were thanked for their time.

Sources of data gathered for this investigation included the STSS (Bride, 2007) as a qualifier, a survey designed for this specific study to collect demographics, in-depth interviews, and the researcher's reflective journal. The results of the STSS were used to identify participants who were experiencing VT; individuals who scored at a 28 or above were asked to participate in the study. Surveys were developed to gather demographic information such as gender, age, agency time, and field years.

Participants were asked to complete the short survey prior to the start of the interview (see Appendix); in-depth interviews were electronically recorded and transcribed. A confidentiality agreement was signed to ensure interview data remained confidential and only released to the researcher. Interviews were conducted in a safe space where the participant feels comfortable enough to speak openly according to their feelings (Ataria, 2014). Participants were provided with a summary of the transcription via email for member checking and validation. Member checking (informant feedback) was conducted to aid with validity, credibility, and transferability (Marshall & Rossman, 2011).

Instruments

The instruments used in this study included the STSS (Bride, 2007), a short survey to gather demographic information, the interview guide which was developed for this study and field tested, and the researcher's reflective journal (see appendix). The STSS (Bride, 2007) was used to measure the subjects' responses to VT within the past week of the time of the interview. It is a screening tool used to identify individuals with VT. The STSS is a 17-piece self-reporting tool to assess the occurrence of specific indicators associated with STS (Bride, 2007).

Prospective participants responded using a five-point Likert scale with scores that ranged from *never* to *very often*, representing which item reflected their experiences of the past week from the date of the survey and/or interview. The phrasing of directives and detailed stressor items were intended so stressors were a revelation to participants (Bride, 2007). A score of 28 and above was used to identify prospective participants who were experiencing VT/STS.

The interviews and journal provided qualitative data which the researcher used to identify patterns and themes. The STSS was established due to the need for instruments that would specifically measure STS/VT indications in social workers and other specialists (Bride et al., 2004). For this study, the cutoff score of 28 was adapted from Bride's (2007) second approach to the interpretation of scores. Bride described three approaches to the interpretation of scores using the STSS. The first approach is using the following algorithm: if a person scored in one item in the intrusion subscale, at least three items in the avoidance scale, and at least two items in the arousal scale, that individual may be experiencing PTSD at a diagnostic level due to STS. Individual scores were shared with participants, and participants with higher scores were provided with appropriate referrals, but were not excluded from the study. The second approach, used in this study, entails a cutoff at a score of 28; individuals with a score less than 28 were interpreted as having little or no STS, scores of 28-37 were considered mild STS, scores of 38-43 were interpreted at moderate STS, and 44-48 were interpreted as high STS (Bride, 2007). The third approach to the interpretation of scores on the STSS resulted from the cutoff value of 28; individuals scoring at a 28 and above were considered to have PTSD due to STS (Bride, 2007). Since the purpose of this study did not involve PTSD, the second approach to the interpretation of scores and STS was utilized.

The STSS has substantiated evidence of convergent, discriminant, and factorial validity and high levels of internal consistency (Bride, 2007; Bride et al., 2004). The tool can be used to commence empirical investigations into the prevention and improvement of STS among mental-health workers and other professionals (Bride et al., 2004). A coefficient alpha was used to assess internal consistency. Means, standard deviations, and alpha levels for the STSS and subscales were as follows. Full STSS (M = 29.49, SD = 10.76, α = .93), Intrusion (M = 8.11, SD = 3.03, α = .80), Avoidance (M = 12.49, SD = 5.0, α = .87) and Arousal (M = 8.89, SD = 3.57, α = .83). Alpha levels between .80 and .90 were considered to be great (Bride et al., 2004). The Bonferroni technique was used to set the Familywise error rate at α = .05, resulting in a per comparison alpha level of 00179 (.05/28) because 28 correlations were prearranged when examining convergent and discriminant validity (Bride et al., 2004). The factorial validity of the STSS was addressed using a confirmatory factor analysis that utilized structural equation modeling SEM techniques and maximum likelihood estimation. LISREL 8.3 software was used for the analysis using a covariance medium (Bride et al., 2004). Bride granted permission to use the STSS as a free-of-charge research tool.

Participants were scheduled to be part of an in-depth interview that was recorded and transcribed. A confidentiality agreement was signed, to ensure participant's transcribed data remained confidential Participants were asked to answer 10 open-ended questions to the best of their ability (Appendix). The interviews were audio recorded and conducted in a safe and confidential space. Patterns and themes were identified through data analysis. These patterns and themes were geared towards answering the research questions. The in-depth interviews generated qualitative data. NVivo 12 software was used for analyzing the qualitative data after codes and categories were identified. When conducting interviews, smaller numbers of participants were used due to the intensity of the interviews and the length of time needed to conduct the interviews.

Using open-ended questions required the subjects to answer questions without using one-word answers and allowed them to share lived experiences in greater depth. Semi-structured interviews involved the use of pre-arranged questions where participants were free to ask for clarification, thus streamlining the collection of comparable categories of information from the participants to generating direction (Doody & Noonan, 2013). The interview questions were field tested by field experts.

A researcher's journal was kept which included all phases of the planning, implementation, and organization of the study, in addition to notes on issues that arose during the interviews. Self-reflection was also an integral part of the journal. This journal information was transcribed and used intermittently in the results section to confirm and serve as affirmation. After each interview, any of the researcher's thoughts, feelings, and impressions related to the interview and the process were documented in the journal.

When describing the research sample, it is advantageous to provide a visual description. Participant demographic information was gathered using a short survey designed for this specific investigation. The information on the survey included gender, age, time at the agency, and time in the profession. A descriptive analysis using IBM SPSS was conducted to describe the sample.

Research Questions

The following question guided this research project and was the core of the investigation: "How do mental-health workers describe coping with vicarious trauma?" A research sub-question was included: "How do mental-health workers use self-care in response to vicarious trauma?"

Data Analysis

Effective analysis of qualitative data requires organization and process that can establish and target meaning (Vaughn & Turner, 2015). Qualitative data analysis involves the analysis of words, forms,

text, and other nonnumerical depictions of information
which may include observation (McDavid, Huse, &
Hawthorn, 2013). Patterns and themes were further
analyzed for understanding and interpretation using
Moustakas' (1994) transcendental phenomenology
process.

Coding was completed by using data derived
from transcripts to identify words and phrases that fit
a certain pattern and form themes. Themes were
labeled with words or codes that allowed the
researcher to answer the research questions as they
became repetitive and were frequently used in the
transcriptions. Specific patterns, themes, and sub-
themes generated by the interviews and journal were
sought to answer the research questions. To
effectively analyze qualitative data, the researcher
needed to incorporate a system and process that
organizes and targets meaning (Vaughn & Turner,
2015). The 12 transcriptions were imported into
NVivo 12 software, where codes and nodes were
identified. A code in qualitative investigations is
mostly a term or short expression that represents a
collective, salient, reality capturing and/or reminiscent
characteristic for a part of dialectal-based or graphic

data (Saldana, 2016). The results from the analysis of the interviews, validated by member checking, and content analysis of the researcher's reflective journal creating a triangulated framework aligning with the research questions.

The SPSS generated a descriptive analysis using data from the survey to provide a description of the sample. Statistical Package for the Social Sciences (SPSS) analysis software is used for interactive statistical analysis. All data was managed and prepared for analysis by the investigator, outcomes were documented in preparation for a detailed written report, and data stored in a locked environment for seven years.

Ethical Considerations

The current research involved VT, also known as STS, experienced by helping professionals encountering (hearing) stories or accounts of harmful experiences shared by their patients. Due to the topic and the trauma involved, the participants were identified as being at a possible psychological risk. Ethical considerations and precautions were taken to ensure participant safety including obtaining approval for the study from the Capella University Institutional Review Board (IRB). Resources were provided or made available to participants, including debriefing and counseling (if requested). Information about the study and participant resources was distributed to participants at the close of the interview. Steps were taken to ensure confidentiality and safekeeping of clients' notes and records. Any potential for psychological harm was mitigated by offering resources such as counseling and employment assistant programs. Participants were provided with time to debrief after the interviews were conducted. Adequate informed consent allowed participants to decide if they wanted to be part of the study, guided by clear and accurate information. It was imperative that all deliberations and procedures are followed to protect and respect the human subjects (Hacker, 2013).

Expected Findings

This research study was geared towards identifying vicarious traumatization and secondary traumatic stress in the daily-lived experiences of workers employed in the field of mental health that serve distressed clients. The goal was to show a need for additional supports to workers in the mental-health profession. Mental-health professionals, educators, policymakers, and other associated organizations may benefit from the expected findings as VT/STS may lead to work complications such as burnout, loss of staff, and unexplained staff absences. By investigating the effects of VT on the overall daily experience, professionals in the mental-health field could potentially be better equipped to manage work-related stress, which may cause internal turmoil or feelings of inadequacy. Vicarious trauma refers to a snowballing of negative effects of working with traumatized clients, which involves interference with the workers feelings, intellectual schemas, worldview memories, effectiveness, and disruption in overall wellness (Dorociak et al., 2017). Vicarious trauma does not represent illness in the worker or the victim, but rather is the passing on of traumatic stress by listening to distressing information (Hernandez-Wolf et al., 2015). Mental-health professionals are exposed to VT daily. There is increased awareness at the importance of self-care in the field of mental health (Dorociak et al., 2017).

Dedicated mental-health professionals are faced with countless numbers of difficulties to be managed to function effectively in the work setting and in everyday lives. These demands may cause great stress that – if not addressed – could have detrimental consequences for service provisions. Work-related threats for delivering services to traumatized and violence exposed individuals could become a public health risk, threatening the workforce balance (Molnar et al., 2017). The process ensuing negative consequences has been compared to a mental or emotional decline (initiated with stress) and unmanageable coping mechanisms, which leads to anguish within the worker (Dorociak et al., 2017). Stress, lack of self-care, and the absence of a culture-of-care within a working organization can be detrimental to the helping profession and the social-work profession. Without a harmonized response from researchers, politicians, and organizational leadership, these helping professionals are abandoned to the collective load of trauma accumulated from lingering and accrued hardship, also known as VT and STS (Molnar et al., 2017).

The researcher anticipated this investigation would contribute to existing literature regarding VT and STS and is expected to add to the body of knowledge by identifying the need for self-care within the profession. The expectations for this study were that outcomes would answer the research questions and the results would reflect previously non-identified levels of VT/STS among the mental-health workers, thereby indicating a need for self-care initiatives. The impact this study has on a worksite will be beneficial to the environment, the population, and the organization's clients. It is unrealistic to expect mental-health workers to be healthy 100% of the time; it is reasonable to expected workers be functional enough to perform effectively. Consideration needs to be given when providing beneficial treatment to clients, which entails the worker be mentally, physically, and spiritually healthy. Self-care needs to be implemented in work settings to provide mental-health workers with additional tools to support work-related stress. According to Dorociak et al. (2017), when workers are healthy outcomes are positive.

The social-work profession holds high regards

to professional standards when providing services to their clients and patients. The mental-health profession teaches social workers that clients are first; and as mentioned in the code of ethics, a social worker's main objective is to serve those in distress, advocate for social issues, and provide service to others in need first and foremost (NASW, 2017; Wheeler & McClain, 2015). Special attention should be directed towards service providers since they are the individuals at the forefront of patient / client care. Moving beyond the deterrence of self or client problems, practical and constant self-care promotes functioning and wellness consequently contributing to an ideal level of professional and personal satisfaction (Zahniser et al., 2017). Research findings have aligned with the research goals of this investigation. The first goal was to establish ongoing self-care monitoring in the workplace environment in response to VT and STS. The second goal was to utilize training and curriculums to improve the quality of health and well-being for the mental-health workers while creating a culture of care within the organization.

Chapter 4

Data Collection and Analysis

Introduction: The Study and the Researcher

This chapter is geared at explaining the collected data, the results of the research study, and other findings. The methods and procedures in the previous chapter were carried out to understand the lived experiences of mental-health workers, VT, and self-care. The understanding of the findings has been presented using a transcendental phenomenological approach. This chapter consists of the researcher's role, background, and what led the research to conducting this study, a discussion of the participant sample, the methodology applied to the data analysis, and the data and results of the analysis. Descriptions of the mental-health workers lived experiences, when dealing with VT, how they experienced it and thoughts about self-care when experiencing it, are included, in addition to the researcher's analysis.

The researcher's role was that of an outsider with collaboration from insiders. The research problem and questions were discussed in meetings with stakeholders. The researcher developed the research questions, had them field tested, and designed the demographic survey specifically for this study. The researcher's role included gathering data, scheduling and conducting interviews, organizing meetings, communicating with stakeholders, transcribing and analyzing data, writing the final detailed report, and preparing the report for dissemination. The researcher had never conducted qualitative research before; personal experience was with utilizing quantitative methods. The researcher felt comfortable conducting the study and was prepared to do so with the guidance of a mentor.

The interest the researcher had in VT and self-care stems from more than 20 years of mental health and social work. The researcher worked with trauma within the researcher's professional career. Some of this experience included working with families of the victims of the World Trade Center (September 11, 2001) disaster and the families of the victims of Flight 587 (November 12, 2001) which crashed shortly after the Trade Center disaster due to mechanical failure. The researcher's work also included working with victims of sexual assault and sexual abuse. Through the researcher' career, there was personally-experienced isolation, sadness, fear, and feelings of inadequacy. There were moments when the researchers questioned work, as well as moments of tiredness, sleeplessness, and overall feelings of being unhealthy. Only after a lot of research and a deeper understanding of the researcher's feelings was the researcher able to come to grips with the feelings a mental-health worker experiences after many years of working with trauma.

As this research has suggested, VT may change workers and the way they look at life, the way they live life, their social schemas, and their personal choices. It affects workers both professionally and personally. The researcher felt this phenomenon needed attention, as many individuals did not know of the term and had no knowledge of the feelings and behaviors associated with it. The researcher felt awareness was needed for this sensitive topic – to identify methods in which organizations, employers and others involved in decision making for the social work profession could prevent VT and treat the helpers. The researcher practiced self-care at times; however, only practiced self-care as a last resort when the researcher felt burned out or when personal health was suffering. The researcher asked, "Why do mental-health workers not practice what we preach? Why are my patients so important, and why was it so easy to put my family aside so I could help others?" The researcher felt that, as a licensed-clinical social worker, it was the researcher's responsibility to self, to all those in the helping profession, and to the researcher's family to bring awareness to this phenomenon. The researcher's goal with this study was to get answers and solutions for mental-health workers; to bring awareness to the issue and add to the existing body of knowledge. This knowledge was obtained by seeking solutions through the lived experiences of other mental-health workers.

Through experience descriptions, the researcher found skill development and understanding. A mental-health worker serves as a good foundation for investigating VT and STS, the researcher also understood, to conduct a fair study, the researcher had to set aside biases and feelings.

As the research was conducted, there were times when the researcher wanted to, and could have, stepped into the helping worker role; however, maintained emotional distance as a professional researcher. This was a challenge, as the temptation was there. As interviews were conducted, there were physical responses. The researcher self-prompted, "I am the researcher, not the clinician or supervisor." Through experience as an administrator, a clinician, and a supervisor … these roles prepared the researcher to be objective. The researcher was aware the role was different; to conduct a successful study the researcher was that, and nothing more.

Description of the Participants

The 12 mental-health workers participating in this research study were recruited from a non-profit community agency with a mental-health component located in a northeastern state. The participants were recruited through an agency staff meeting. Initially, two of the prospective participants did not score at 28 or above on the STSS; therefore, the recruitment process continued until 12 participants were recruited.

Out of the 12 participants that met the inclusion criteria score, one chose not to move on with the study, requiring the recruitment of another participant. The participant that chose to not move on gave no specific reason why the decision was made. For this study, the cutoff score of 28 was adapted from Bride's (2007) second approach to the interpretation of scores of the STSS. Bride described three approaches to the interpretation of scores using the STSS. The first approach used the following algorithm: if the individual scores in at least one item in the intrusion subscale, at least three items in the avoidance scale, and at least two items in the arousal scale, that individual may be experiencing PTSD at a diagnostic level due to STS. The second approach, used in this study, entails a cutoff at a score of 28; individuals with less than 28 are interpreted as little or no STS, scores of 28-37 are considered mild STS, scores of 38-43 are interpreted at moderate STS, and 44-48 are interpreted as high STS (Bride, 2007). The third approach to the interpretation of scores on the STSS is by establishing a cutoff value of 38; therefore, individuals scoring at a 38 and above would be considered to have PTSD due to STS (Bride,

2007). Since the purpose of this study did not involve PTSD, the researcher chose the second approach to the interpretation of scores and STS.

The 12 participants in this study were all females and lived in the state; the only male who expressed interest was one of the prospective participants that did not score within the inclusion criteria. The participants were ages 28-62 years old. Their lengths of time at the agency ranged from three months to 20 years, and their years in the field ranged from two years to 35 years. To describe the sample, a descriptive analysis was conducted using SPSS (Table 1).

Table 1 - Demographics

	N	M	SD	Minimum	Maximum	Median
Gender	12	38.58	11.35	28	62	34.50
Age	12					
Time in the Agency (Years)	12	4.79	5.42	0.25	20.00	3.50
Years in the Field	12	11.00	8.82	2.00	35.00	9.00

The participants were asked to fill out a paper survey which included demographic data before the start of the interviews. Demographics would identify if anyone not included in the research (interviews, questions, surveys) jeopardized the confidentiality, safety, and privacy of a participant. The demographics used were age, gender, time at the agency, and time in the field. In referring to the participants, the pronouns she, her, and herself may be used for simplification of communication and anonymity. Participants were assigned a participant "P" number from one to 12 for confidentiality. Confidentiality, safety, and privacy were monitored throughout the study as well as repeatedly stated that anyone could excuse themselves from the study at any time. The research site was also assured repeatedly of the steps being taken to maintain confidentiality and safety before, during, and after the research.

The participants were all respectful and well versed. A few were nervous in the beginning, but became comfortable soon after rapport was established. Interviews were double-taped in case one of the recorders failed.

Research Methodology Applied
to the Data Analysis

The method of analysis in this investigation follows Moustakas' (1994) transcendental phenomenology path of analysis. The phenomenological approach incorporates a revisit to experience to recapture detailed imageries that provide the core for a thoughtful structural analysis that represent the hearts of the moment (Moustakas, 1994). Using Moustakas' transcendental phenomenology approach, the preliminary findings of these repeated patterns and themes were followed by reduction and elimination. The reduction and elimination were determined by whether the expression contained a moment of experience, and whether that moment was sufficiently understood. Moustakas (1994) posited phenomenology as a suitable instrument for discovering and unfolding collective experiences associated to the phenomena.

When using transcendental phenomenology, the following process is followed, initially starting with the epoche. Epoche is when all prejudgments are set aside, and the discussion opens with an unprejudiced

and receptive presence (Moustakas, 1994). The
second, core process, is a transcendental-
phenomenological reduction, and the third core
process is imaginative variation, which refers to
looking for possible meanings with imagination,
different frames of reference, and a variety of
perspectives (Moustakas, 1994).

Rich data from the participants' transcripts
were used to identify emerging patterns and themes
to condense into codes and nodes. NVivo data
coding software explores data for developing
patterns, which are then analyzed for recurring
themes using word and text query for analysis (QSR
International, 2016). The data analyzed by NVivo
software were then checked for accuracy and
interpretations of meanings. A manual review of the
data organized by the NVivo software was also
conducted to quality for accuracy. The findings were
analyzed and interpreted in search for meaning and
answers to the research questions.

The following steps were taken using NVivo
data-coding software to organize qualitative data into
categories: (a) themes developed from manual
identification and analysis of data using the interview

instrument protocol and alignment to address research questions; (b) themes developed and entered as Nodes; (c) folders created and data (interviews, journal) imported (internal folder); (d) tools set up to code data into proper nodes folders; (e) rich and descriptive data coded; (6) words and text queries checked for compatibility of themes and frequency of data terms; and (f) coded data manually quality assured for verification.

All participants arrived as scheduled, rapport was established by introductions, explanation of the process, and testing the recording devices. Participants were given opportunity to ask questions' confidentiality and safety were verbally addressed once again.

Presentation of the Data and
Results of the Analysis

The research question that guided this investigation was, "How do mental-health workers describe coping with vicarious trauma?" The research sub-question was, "How do mental-health workers use self-care in response to vicarious trauma?"

The 12 participants in this study were identified as having VT by scoring a 28 or above on the qualifying instrument (STSS). The results demonstrate patterns and themes that identify mental-health workers and experienced with VT. The workers voiced being affected at varying levels which may have to do with the length of time in the field, their own personal history of trauma, or their support system. There is a disconnect between workers who experienced VT, their personal self-care, and the level of mental-health workers' understanding of the meaning of self-care.

The STSS (Bride, 2007) was used to measure the subjects' responses to VT in the past week from the date of the interview. For this study, the cutoff score of 28 was adapted from Bride's second approach to the interpretation of scores (Bride, 2007). Table 2 presents the STSS scores based on levels of intrusion, avoidance, and arousal. Any participant with a total score of 28 or above was considered to have STS. Participants scored between 32 and 66. The scores were used for qualification to participate in the study. Participants were informed of their scores.

Table 2 - Secondary Traumatic Stress Scale Scores

Participant	Intrusion	Avoidance	Arousal	Total
P1	22	23	21	66
P2	17	27	20	64
P3	11	16	13	40
P4	06	12	14	32
P5	11	14	11	36
P6	10	15	09	34
P7	07	18	15	40
P8	18	23	15	56
P9	14	13	15	42
P10	21	27	18	66
P11	09	17	16	42
P12	17	19	17	53

Emerging themes were developed from the rich data collected from the transcribed interviews with participants. The interview sessions consisted of recorded interviews using 10 open-ended questions (Appendix). Any response from any question could fit into any formed concept/theme and pattern; many responses were specific. The analysis presented outcomes of the queries. The findings yielded four core themes and 12 sub-themes.

1. Core Theme: Workplace Factors
   1a) Experiences of Mental Health Workers
   1b) Feelings of Inadequacy

2. Core Theme: Client Interactions

    2a) Identifying with Client Issues

    2b) Clinical Notes and Documentation

3. Core Theme: Stress Factors

    3a) Managing Stress and Coping with Anxiety on
    the Job

    3b) Physical Symptoms and Coping Mechanisms

    3c) Prolonged Experiences Associated with
    Situational Thoughts

4. Core Theme: Self-Care Factors

    4a) Self-Care Defined

    4b) Workplace Support of Self-Care

    4c) Activities to Engage Self-Care

    4d) Support Systems Available

    4e) Suggestions to Improve Activities

The participants described lived experiences associated with work as mental-health workers and answered interview questions. Once interviews were concluded, participants were provided with time to debrief. All transcriptions were sent to participants for member checking. The Nvivo 12 software was an asset to categorizing data under each arranged theme. Table 3 depicts four core themes and 12 sub-themes associated under each core theme. This table represents the emerging core themes and sub-themes from the data analysis. The letter (*n*) defines the total mention of themes by any participant during all interviews (Table 3).

Table 3 - *The Frequency of Core and Sub-themes Mentioned During Interviews*

Core Themes (4) Sub-themes (12)	Participant Influence	*n*
1) Core Theme: Workplace Factors		
1a) Experiences of Mental Health Workers	12	24
1b) Feelings of Inadequacy	12	24
2) Core Theme: Client Interactions		
2a) Identifying with Client Issues	12	37
2b) Clinical Notes and Documentation	2	2
3) Core Theme: Stress Factors		
3a) Managing Stress and Coping with Anxiety on the Job	12	43
3b) Physical Symptoms and Coping Mechanisms	12	28
3c) Prolonged Experiences Associated with Situational Thoughts	12	32
4) Core Theme: Self-care Factors		
4a) Self-care Defined	12	17
4b) Work Place Support of Self-care	12	24
4c) Activities to Engage Self-care	12	20
4d) Support Systems Available	12	29
4e) Suggestions to Improve Activities	12	24

Core Theme 1: Workplace Factors

In the workplace, when working with trauma patients, the amount of stress and trauma experienced and the accounts of worker's stories may take a toll on the mental-health-care providers, which may lead to the worker experiencing VT/STS. All 12 participants mentioned the workplace stress and challenges as they highlighted work experiences. Core theme 1 answers questions 1 and 6 of the interview guide (Appendix).

In the treatment of trauma patients in clinical settings, the workplace has several elements that factor in how mental-health workers perceive their experiences, and how these interactions may produce as emotionally, challenging, and stressful. Workplace factors such as intensity of the work, administrative demands, deadlines, and emotional challenges were identified. Workplace factors have been identified as a core theme, and two sub-themes emerged from the interviews. The first sub-theme identified was the lived experiences of mental-health workers in their workplaces, and the second sub-theme was inadequacy at the workplace. In phenomenology, the lived and shared experiences of participants are crucial in exploring the gaps in knowledge pertaining to how they reflect on their experiences (Donalek, 2004).

For example, P10 said,

> My experience as a mental-health worker ... I can say ... that throughout these years I have been working in the mental-health field for eight years ... has been draining. It has taken a toll on me. It makes me view life differently. It ... I can say that it really breaks me as a person. I don't think that I was ever prepared so ... I don't think anyone is ever prepared to work in a mental-health field. I think it just so happens that you want to make a change and it's such a great field and you come in with a vision and then sometimes throughout time your vision dwindles because of what you go through and what you hear and

the situations and the scenarios. Yes.
For example, I came into the mental-
health field thinking I am going to rescue
everyone. Rescue everyone from being
homeless. Rescue a child from being
abused. Rescue a person from not
committing suicide. Like I had the
magical wand. Then, what I have
encountered throughout these years is
that sometimes I do not have anything in
my hands to save someone. Or, I do
not have the capability to provide the
person what they need. Here I am with
this vision I am going to save everyone
… and I cannot. They will still get
abused. Or, they will still be homeless.
Or, they might go hungry … and that
really takes a toll on me.

P11 noted,

Overwhelming. Stressful at times.
There is always a lot to do. There is
always a need. There is not always the

support. I do the best I can. There are
always more clients than there are
clinicians; so, you get overwhelmed with
the work that you're given when it
comes to just direct client care. And,
then on top of that, it is what is required
of the agency. Paperwork, meetings,
things we must log in. I guess regular
things that make the agency stay afloat
for them. There is always something to
do, so you're always trying to find the
balance between the paperwork side of
the agency, the meetings, and whatever
they're requiring for me to do, as well as
taking care of the clients themselves.

P12 mentioned,

My experience as a mental-health
worker has been stressful. I have been
in the field for many years. The work
itself has influenced me personally, as
well as professionally. I work with a
population that has a lot of trauma.

They are ... parents ... they are under a lot of stress. I have worked in many areas within the field, with families, and children. People experiencing hard challenges, that in turn affect me, as a worker. This work has been so stressful that I have experienced issues with stress, and sometimes depression ... it is very difficult to deal with the system. Fighting with them, going in there and advocating for them is very difficult. It has been a very difficult road. It is taking a long time. You must go in there and advocate for your client and that makes me feel angry at times, very frustrated. It is very difficult for me. I get very stressed out when I deal with providers like that. I am talking about the court system, I am talking about school. It's ... frustrating for me and it is very stressful. I take all that home. The frustration ... I take it home. Sometimes I take it out on my kids ... I take it out on my husband, because I don't know what

to do. I tried my best and still, my best
sometimes is not enough to help our
population.

**Sub-theme 1a: Experiences of mental-
health workers**. STS and VT are terms used
interchangeably that describe the consequences of
secondary traumatic exposure. These experiences
may affect service providers in unusual ways, thereby
affecting their daily work. Individuals working in the
field of trauma, victim services, mental health (e.g.,
social workers), police force, fire response,
emergency services, and other professionals are
exposed to distressing events every day (Molnar et
al., 2017). Participants shared their most appropriate
responses while considering and reflecting on what
the question asked. Work experiences were
described as hard, challenging, stressful, and
overwhelming. These are the highlights of
participants from their responses.

P1 mentioned,

I have worked with mandated clients, I

have worked with substance abuse, I
have worked in intensive outpatient
programs, I have worked as a
community support specialist, I have
worked in the intake. But right now, the
last two years, I have been working in a
trauma program for domestic violence
and sexual assault, so what I am seeing
is a lot of clients who have acute stress
symptoms, as well as victimizations of
crime and sexual assault and abuse,
and I am doing individual therapy, and
group therapy. We are doing case
management and working as advocates,
going to court to help them through their
court cases where they do not have
other supports in understanding the
court system. We also do film series
and book clubs for the clients that are a
little bit intimidated by the group therapy
or therapy in general, but it kind of
softens what it means to go to therapy
… for them. My work is hard and
challenging.

P2 mentioned,

> I supervise clinicians who are providing
> mental health care, and I also provide
> therapy services to families, and
> children, and adults. I have been doing
> this probably for the last 12 years. First,
> I did just outpatient children. And then
> for the last five years, I have been at this
> agency. It is hard work, very hard and
> stressful.

P3 noted,

> Well, it has been enriching because I
> like what I do. I am also in a lot of
> stress and anxiety because the
> population that I work with is a
> population with a lot of trauma,
> problems and have a lot of needs and
> which is probably the reasons they have
> mental health problems. We have
> clients that come from different

backgrounds, they have different
experiences, so my work is very
stressful … very, and I have a lot of
anxiety, but it also has been very
enriching, you know I like what I do. I
have doing this job for about 10 years. I
have worked with children, teenagers
and now adults. I have worked with
people that have been physically,
emotionally and sexually abused,
minorities, people who are
oppressed…and that is very hard and
eventually, it takes a toll on you. You go
home thinking … how is your client
sleeping, eating…is he or she being
abused at this moment? You wish you
could do more.

P4 mentioned,

Since I have been in the field it has
been interesting and challenging as I
have had some rewarding moments, but
I have had some overwhelming

situations that I did not know how to
cope with them being that this is my first
experience in the field.

Sub-theme 1b: Feelings of inadequacy.
Question 6 opened an opportunity for the mental-
health workers to share feelings of inadequacy at
related to work. Mental-health workers help clients
with challenges that consequently have a negative
impact on their own daily lives (Branson et al., 2014;
Figley, 1999). Consequently, these issues may be
co-occurring with a history of trauma (Branson et al.,
2014). Through the nature of their work, mental-
health workers may find themselves unable to provide
inadequate treatment to the clients, leaving them
feeling stressed and challenged. Feelings of
inadequacy, not doing enough, not helping enough,
not knowing what to do, and desires for more training
came up. Mental-health workers are particularly
vulnerable to burnout due to VT, to the extent the
workers question the meaning of their work, feel loss
of purpose, and feel hopeless, due to the
internalization of the suffering of their clients' traumas
(Dombo & Gray, 2013). These are highlights of the

participants shared experiences.

P10 noted,

> Inadequacy would be in the sense of the
> type of work I am providing. Because I
> really feel that given the circumstance, I
> can offer a lot more to the clients, but
> given my work environment, because I
> am doing so much that I am really am
> not focusing where I want to focus. In
> case management or helping the clients,
> like my mission, was. To come in and
> save … 'save them.' I am not focusing
> on that because I am focusing on other
> aspects of the program. My mission of
> coming in, in general to mental health I
> am not even – I am not really
> accomplishing that. I feel I am
> inadequate in that. I feel like I am not
> saving anyone. I cannot focus on that
> as much because I am focusing on
> other things, so I feel that my work is
> inadequate. And as for me, inadequacy

with myself at work because I am not
doing what I know I can do. To the full
ability. I feel like I am just a waste of
potential.

P12 noted,

> For me, it is when I cannot get … help
> for them. Especially when families are
> being evicted and you cannot do
> anything about it. There is no place to
> go, families do not want to take them in,
> and you cannot do anything because
> there is no place to go. It is very
> difficult. Or if they are turning off the
> light in the winter time, or the gas, and
> you cannot do anything because I do
> not have $7,000 to give the gas
> company. Our program does not do
> that. And it is the last-minute thing, and
> the client has nowhere to go. I feel
> inadequate. I feel that I have not done
> my job and it is very difficult to go home
> to this situation and knowing that she is

in the house with no heat, and she
cannot cook. To me, it is very difficult. I
feel down, I feel like I have not done my
job. And you know, sometimes you cry.
You cannot help it. You cry because
you cannot do anything and it is very
difficult, even when you call people,
even when you call their family and they
do not, help … they say, 'Oh, no. That
is on her. Nobody told her not to pay
the bill.' And there are kids. What are
you going to do? And there is nothing
you really can do because we just do
not have money to pay for a gas bill that
big. So, it is very difficult.

P2 shared,

How much can we do? What can we
do? And so, there is this sense of
feeling helpless, like there is nothing we
can do, because it is really up to this
person and whatever resources they
have, to make a decision and say, I do

not want to live a life like this anymore.
So, so that makes me feel like, are we
doing enough? Are we doing enough?
Are we doing enough? I do not know if
we are doing enough.

P3 stated,

Oh [laughter] that happens often. I
sometimes feel like I cannot help the
client the way I want to help because
either I do not have the experience, or
the agency does not have the means to
help that client; who that client needs
more intensive, more ongoing therapy
and sometimes I cannot provide it
because of the case-load. I feel
sometimes I need more training, I need
more guidance, in terms of supervision
sometimes mostly because everybody is
so busy. I make excuses for the people
but yeah, I feel that way often, many
times I feel that I could have done or do
more but then I don't have the time or
the means.

Core Theme 2: Client Interaction

In trauma work, the client and worker interaction are primarily the main cause of VT/STS. Vicarious trauma refers to the negative snowballing effect of working with traumatized clients, involving interference with the therapist's feelings, cognitive schematics, worldly recollections, self-efficacy, and sense of wellness (Dorociak et al., 2017). Secondary traumatic stress denotes behaviors and emotions after helping a traumatized or anguished individual (Caringi et al., 2017; Fingley, 1995). During their work, mental-health professionals (e.g., social workers) are exposed to an enormous amount of traumatic experiences raised by their patients / clients (Halevi & Idisis, 2017). As a result, workers are experiencing noteworthy reactions. Mental-health workers shared these experiences as they identified with client issues. Feelings of fear, pain, and stress were shared when identifying with clients. Core theme 2 answers interview question 5 (see Appendix). All 12 workers identified with client issues because of their own personal trauma.

P1 mentioned,

> I experienced a lot of trauma in my life, I
> stayed away, and I was terrified. But
> then, I decided if I want to be the best
> clinician I can be, I need to be able to
> help people who are in trauma
> situations, rather than trying to stay
> away. I went into this program and I
> actually found that this is where I
> belong, and this is where I'm the most
> effective clinician, and as far as relating
> to them, I have experienced a lot of
> domestic violence. I have experienced
> sexual assault as a child, and as an
> adult. I have actually experienced
> workplace violence. I was working
> somewhere where there was a stabbing.
> I was standing next to a man who
> stabbed our front-desk person and for a
> long time, I had trauma symptoms
> where I heard a fire truck and I would
> jump, because there were so many

responders and fire trucks at that time.
As far as relating to them, I know what
they are feeling. I know what they have
been through. I know what works and
what does not work for myself, so when
I see them going through something and
they may be kind of hesitant about
something, I have an understanding of
why. I know that it is okay to change our
treatment to meet their needs and what
they are comfortable with, and I have
been able to be effective to help them
with alternatives and other things to do.

P10 mentioned,

As soon as I try to be the professional
and think like, well, you are being
possessive and that is an abuse, a
sense of abuse, and that is mental
abuse and what you are doing is just so
unhealthy, and I could see why she
wants to get out. I went through that. I
had a possessive ex-boyfriend which led

into a bigger situation that I had … the things that he was stating to me were the signs that I was going through and what I lived. It brought me back with I was trying to be a professional and try to understand him, but I didn't want to understand him because he reminded me of my ex. That caused me so much pain and so much agony and so much … everything that went with that situation at that moment I was not a professional in my mind. I would never see that client the same again because he reminds me of my ex-boyfriend. I see him, and it bothers me and at that moment I am … was able to be aware; 'listen, he is not your ex-boyfriend … let it go and treat the client for whatever you're treating.' You're having this dialogue or whatever you are having … it was very hard for me to provide the service because, in reality, I did not want to understand what he was saying. Because for me that is abuse. And for

me, that is what I lived, and I struggled
with that. So since then, someone else
obviously is seeing that person cause, I
cannot. I would never see the client the
same.

Often, professionals have also suffered
trauma, and their personal history may lay
(unrecognized) behind denial and professionalism
(Molnar et al., 2017). Without proper attention, these
workers are being left defenseless to the collective
burden of trauma accumulated from chronic or acute
hardship (Molnar et al., 2017). If not addressed these
professionals may suffer further damage, resulting in
job loss, resignation, or burnout.

**Sub-theme 2a: Identifying with client
issues.** Other factors that may influence vicarious
traumatization in the worker is the worker's own past
experiences of trauma, the significance of traumatic
life events, their emotional wellness, their personal
style, their professional growth, their stressors, and
their personal support system (Pearlman & Maclan,
1995). The following are participants' responses as

they shared experiences identifying with client issues.
The issues they discussed included domestic
violence, suicidal attempts, inability to meet basic
needs, and child abuse.

P11 shared,

> Just trying to get like a service put on
> and given the runaround and having to
> jump through hoops and barrels to get
> something like the gas on or something
> like that. I can identify with that. I went
> through something similar when I came
> to this country.

P12 mentioned,

> I had a client a while back, where it was
> like my family. She had eight kids, did
> not speak English, and did not know
> anything about the community. And to
> me, I felt like it was my childhood back
> … because I have 10 other siblings …
> and I felt this woman was in the same

situation as my father was and I was there. I had to be the one to help them and get the situation done. And it was, for me, being eight years old again and doing that. That is how I felt when I saw this woman with eight kids and not being able to have food or not be able to pay her light bill. And then not speak the language. It was very difficult.

P2 shared,

A while back ... the family since were removed ... with the help of the Department of Children and Families and a domestic violence shelter. They were removed from the perpetrator ... actually moved away. At the time I remembered recently this case where I knew that the domestic violence was going on, that it was active. The mother will deny, but there was a six-year-old that was there that actually got hit in the car, in the midst of mom and dad

physically struggling with each other.
Being from a home where I also
witnessed domestic violence, so that
makes it really hard. Because I have to
put that part of me, that might have
been when I was six at one time and
also saw some things that I could not
control, or, or, you know. So that is hard
… and I try to actually … if I can avoid it.
I try not to take on cases where
domestic violence is the primary issue.
Yeah, so yeah. So, it is hard. It is really
hard. I mean we do it, right? Because
our heart is there, and we want to do it,
but it is hard.

P9 shared,

In the past, maybe five years ago, I went
through…a broken relationship, so that
person cheated on me and he was, not
throughout the relationship, but since he
started seeing that person, he was
verbally abusive and emotionally

abusive. I went through a lot after that. I went through depression. I went to therapy for that. I might have tried to take my life for that because … not because he cheated on me, but because there was sexual assaults and more sickness involved, so I tried to take my life [away] at that time. So, when I have a client that is going through something like that and I am trying to be there for that person, it really gets to me, and I can really go back and relate to that. And how can I tell this person not to do the same thing I did if I already did it? How?

P4 noted,

I had a parent come in with both her children into the office and ... I might get emotional over it because it's just one of those things that it just continues to touch me no matter how long I think about it. But, she walked in with both her children … her older daughter and her younger son. I was supposed to triage her to get her going and I saw the children, everything seemed calm … mom seemed a bit defensive, so I thought I was going to have a difficult time just talking with her. When the children left the office, she told me her daughter's father had touched her son. That was an emotional situation for me, because I think of my children. Sometimes you don't even know what to do, that you don't do anything. With that, that was my very first situation and it was hard. But, after I cried about it, I talked about it, and then I kind of continued to pray for her. I am more vigilant with my children.

Sub-theme 2b: Clinical notes and documentation. Participants P2 and P6 shared that writing clinical notes made them relive the trauma again. Studies have mentioned VT /STS and how mental-health workers are affected by reliving participants' accounts of the stories; however, this was another level of a trauma experience.

P2 shared,

> Because doing the clinical notes means I am going to relive this session where they told me A, B, and C. So that, you know, it is hard because as you know, there is requirements and mandates.

P6 shared,

> I do not want to write this note. Why do I have to relive this thing again to get it out on paper? But, that is the only way to document it, so I struggle with that.

Core Theme 3: Stress Factors

Core theme 3 answers questions 2, 3, and 4 on the interview guide (Appendix). Practicing mental-health practitioners encounter countless numbers of demands to be managed to perform effectively in the

workplace and in their personal lives (Molnar et al.,
2017). These demands may cause great stress that –
if not addressed – may have negative consequences
on the services they provide (Tavormina & Clossey,
2015). Occupational threats for delivering services to
distressed and violence exposed individuals becomes
a hazard, threatening the workforce equilibrium and
the worker's health (Molnar et al., 2017). Demands
that cause stress and anxiety on the job were
expressed as listening to accounts of trauma and the
inability to manage stress and anxiety.

P1 mentioned,

>My job, because we are a trauma
>program, clients come any time, any
>day. The phone rings, and we are a
>hotline, and we are responding to those
>stress calls on a fly, and we are on call
>all the time. Sometimes we have to take
>our phones home and we are on call,
>and that part of my job is stressful
>because it's on 24/7, no matter what, so
>I am always ready, and I am always on

alert and ready for that intense
emotional response from clients.
Because all of these clients coming in
with the trauma symptoms, sometimes
they come in, well … we use self-report
skills. A self-report skill we use is on a
scale of one to 10, where they rate their
symptoms, and that is usually anxiety,
depression, and anger, one through 10,
with 10 being the most severe. A lot of
them are coming in at eight or nine or
10:00 [at night]. Most of the time, we
are working for de-escalation and trying
to bring that number down throughout
therapy, and that is the goal because it
is a short-term program. Because it is a
short-term program, that means that we
are always in the stressful zone, and the
levels are high, so a lot of that causes a
lot of stress and anxiety as well, for me.
A client will come in and she just got
raped, but thinks she was drugged, and
she has no idea and she does not know
what to do, and she did not go for a

doctor's appointment, so right then and there, we have to give her education. We have to make a safety plan. We have to ask her if she wants to go to the doctor if she wants to do a police report. There are so many different steps before we actually do the job of therapy, so it is always just one thing after another and really responding to the client to meet their needs. I am a human, so, as a human, when we are in that zone with them and trying to help them, it also brings up our stress and anxiety levels as well.

P2 shared,

So stressed, and anxiety comes, in different ways. For example, you know when cases are presented and they are very, full of trauma and full of, you know, negative things, or things that we cannot kind of help um, that is obviously out of our control ... we try our best, right, but you know, the case is the case. Those cases come to me through the clinicians, right? So that sometimes is a source of stress and anxiety. You know, am I helping the clinician enough? Are they not, you know … are they going to be able to, to move on and move the case and, also you know, how about their own well-being? The other source of kind of anxiety, stress, comes with certain cases. For me, it is hard when there is domestic violence in the, in the cases. That, for me, is a source of stress and anxiety. It is hard to let them go. You are always thinking, you know, when these people leave my office, are they going to be safe? You hear so many things on the news, you know, that there is like a murder-suicide, and I run to the TV to see. And I pray, oh my god, I hope it is not so-and-so. So that is one thing. And then when there are kids involved, you know, and even with DCF involved, and all this other you know, "safety things" that they put in

place. I know that there is always that

level of risk, and so that, that gives me,

that gives me more anxiety and stress.

Sub-theme 3a: Managing stress and coping with anxiety on the job. Managing stress and coping with anxiety at the job may have negative consequences that may affect service provision. This may affect a worker's health emotionally and physically. Research question 2 (Appendix) opened the platform for participants to share their thoughts. Mental-health workers shared descriptions associated with the stress and anxiety at work that resulted in physical as well as emotional responses, lack of sleep, an increase in anxiety and stress, and an overall feeling of hopelessness. These are the highlights of the participants' experiences.

P10 shared,

I do not handle it very well. I do not. I

do not think I know how to handle it. I

try to cope the best I can, but I do not

think at this moment in my life that I can take any more stress. I have a lot. I have a lot on my plate. With my population of work that I do, it is an extremely fast-paced program. I have severely big substance abusers. They were in the criminal justice system. Because I came in – with the only one with the experience of the program, it is like I have taken the program on my shoulders. By making sure the clients are well, the program is functioning and how to help my supervisor manage the program. See the bigger picture of the program or look into the drug screens to see if we could save that person from an overdose and there is not a lot of areas of expertise in substance abuse. I am constantly stressed by the fast-paced program. I am constantly stressed about helping everyone to keep afloat. I am constantly stressed with the clients that they might overdose or commit a crime because we are not being cautious or providing the correct service or even knowing, what was the correct service. For me, it is a lot of stress because in my mind we are being negligent. That for me, I cannot sleep at night. That gives me so much stress. Not only for the client but for the agency too. I am always continuously working like I am going to save a program. And, I do not know how to cope with it.

P3 shared,

Working with clients that have suffered from trauma, have been sexually abused, or a client in a situation that is really hard to escape, it is really hard to get out, it is hard to help them. It is just really stressful I feel … sometimes I cannot help much. There are so many problems that the changes that you can make, or that the client make, are very little. So, that creates a lot of anxiety, a lot of frustration.

P4 shared,

> Typically, the stress that comes from
> work is when some situations are
> treated as a priority and others are not.
> When clients are being treated unfairly
> and as a worker of the agency you
> should not call them out because it is
> unprofessional, that is the most
> overwhelming circumstances that the
> agency has made me feel. Makes me
> feel hopeless.

P5 mentioned,

> Actually, this is a funny question
> because this field, it is becoming more
> and more stressful due to everything
> that is going on in the world. One of the
> things is as a professional in this field,
> for me, I really do not want to let my
> clients know I am stressed. I manage it
> very well. I am really calm. I do not try

to show when things. If we are late for
an appointment or things are out of
whack, I always try to maintain my
calmness because I do not want them to
be riled up. How I handle it, is I really
try to put it on the back burner and pick
it up when I get out of work. That can
cause a lot of anxiety and stress for me
as a mental-health worker.

P6 shared,

Currently, I am having a hard time with
just wanting to be effective. I do not
know if that is my own stuff that I am
bringing to the job, but always want to
make sure that with all my clients I want
to be effective. I want to make a
difference, otherwise I do not see the
point in it. What I find stress in, is when
I have clients that sometimes they do
not want to do the work. Sometimes
they do not want to deal with having
appointments and sometimes I get

stressed out and frustrated because I
am like, but … I am coming to you. You
do not have to even come, and you are
not paying for it. I am pouring into and
for sessions sometimes I am buying
food and you do not want to do this
thing and you know your kid really
needs it and the kid wants to do it but
…but you cannot say that, so it is
stressful. And then, with clients – to
really drive the point home – you have
to, you have to really ask the questions
and hear what they have to say. It is
hard to hear it because now you have
the visual images in your head [that you]
… they are burned into your memory so
what do you do with that after? You
scream. You go talk to a co-worker.
You do something, but it is hard,
because sometimes with the timing you
have to go to the next appointment

P7 mentioned,

> Oh yes, it is very stressful. Anxiety ... I
> do get a lot of anxiety while I am at
> work. I just kind of push it to the side
> and move on with my day. I have a lot
> of things to do, I have a checklist of my
> day, and I just have to put my anxiety to
> the side and just get on with the day. I
> guess I do not deal with it. I would say
> the complexity of different situations.
> One given day could be a regular day.
> And then, another day, we could have a
> crisis over the phone. The crisis could
> be anything from someone wanting to
> commit suicide or somebody coming
> physically into the office, having a
> mental breakdown. And ... frequently
> this causes me anxiety and stress.

Sub-theme 3b: Physical symptoms and coping mechanisms. Question 3 (Appendix) allowed participants to share the physical symptoms associated with the job experience. VT/STS may lead

to physical and psychological difficulties (Dombo &
Gray, 2013). Physical symptoms described were
headaches, heart palpitations, nightmares, chest pain,
depression, lack of appetite, stress, inability to sleep,
crying, shoulder pain, anxiety, and restless legs. This
may lead to absenteeism and avoidance on the part
of the worker. Over time, VT continues to be a
concern when looking at mental-health workers and
how this phenomenon affects their daily professional
and personal lives. Participants' highlighted
examples follow.

P1 shared,

> Over the last two years, mostly, I have
> been experiencing ... I have
> experienced nightmares. Sometimes, I
> go home and have nightmares. I will
> dream about the clients and in the last
> couple of months, I have been having
> some heart palpitations. I actually feel
> the pain, like it feels like sharp pains
> every day, to the point of where I feel
> like I am having a heart attack. Then,

that leads to me not being able to
breathe as much, so I have to kind of
monitor my heart rate and kind of bring
myself down and use some of the
grounding skills I have ... sometimes I
am not eating as well as I want [to be]. I
used to eat 5-6 small meals a day, and
now I am not even as hungry as I used
to be. They are not directly related to
what clients may be telling me, but then,
a lot of times, I find myself being
chased. It is usually after I talk to a client
who has told me about a domestic
violence situation or where they are
trying to get escape [from], so I am
assuming the dream means I am
escaping, like the client has described to
me, but a lot of it is kind of dark and
always trying to find that escape.

P10 mentioned,

I do not cope with them. I do not know
how ... I ... on a daily basis, my chest

hurts. My chest is heavy all day long. All day long. Before I come to work, I have to literally pause before turning out of the highway before coming into work to process 'okay, today is going to be a good day, everything is going to be fine' and pause before I come into work. Because I know I am going to -- I'm not very happy where I am right now, and I do not know how to cope. I go on my lunch break in a park in hopes I can breathe in and breathe out, so my chest can feel alleviated with that amount of stress and how I am rushed all the time. Oftentimes, I do cry and come back and try to shut up and continue to produce. I continue to work because at the end of the day there is an exception you have to, continue working. Because I just try to brush it off and continue working ... I am never coping with anything.

P11 shared,

> Sometimes I have headaches. I cope
> with them with sometimes taking
> medication. I do not like to take
> medication every day, so I do not. But
> when it gets too severe, I do.
> Sometimes it is due to lack of sleep.
> You eventually get to the point where
> you have got to call out sick, because
> your body is run down. That is what
> ends up happening. Always trying to
> catch up with work. Bringing the work
> home because of deadlines. Notes …
> got to get them in within 48 hours. Lack
> of understanding or remorse of
> management. They want what they
> want. I do as many notes as I can, but it
> leads me to get lack of sleep. I kind of
> suffer in that way. I try to pay it no mind.
> I just do what I got to do to keep just
> enough ahead to not get in a … like a
> write-up situation.

P12 mentioned,

> I experience different things if we talk
> about physical symptoms. I have had
> anything from nightmares to anxiety,
> stress, and depression. I know this has
> to do with the families I work with and
> the stories they share. At this time, I get
> very anxious when I am going to come
> to work. My anxiety level, it is very high.
> Sometimes I get depressed because
> sometimes I just do not want to come
> back to work. That is how difficult,
> sometimes, things are. I just get very
> stressed out a lot of times.

P2 shared,

> So sometimes, headaches. Or
> sometimes that … the heart beating
> faster because you are anticipating, you
> know that is … and again, we know that
> that is a sign of anxiety. Not necessarily
> … my heart is very healthy. It is not a

heart condition. You know, so you
know, there is like these palpitations,
right? That comes through in these
cases, in anticipation. When the days
are hard, that is usually some of the
reactions I have.

P3 noted,

Physical symptoms I get sometimes,
pain on my shoulder, that is where I get
all my stress, on my shoulders.
Sometimes I get a lot of pain, very
uncomfortable. I do not know, I guess a
physical symptom [is I] tend to eat a lot,
overeat just because I get so anxious,
and I think that is it. I get headaches
sometimes, I do not know ... a lot of
problems sleeping sometimes.

**Sub-theme 3c: Prolonged experiences
associated with situational thoughts**. Often,
mental-health workers are the first to listen to a
traumatic experience shared by the victim. If the

mental-health worker is not prepared to listen to their patients and articulate their patient's detached or partially remembered experiences, they may, in turn, dissociate the experiences themselves, leaving them vulnerable and open to unexpected, intrusive, and often unexplained reactions, not only in the professional arena, but in their everyday lives (Boulanger, 2016). Question 4 (Appendix) allowed the participants to share what they think of situations at work after the workday has ended; what follows is what they shared. Situations they shared included feelings of guilt, not wanting to return to work, and not having done enough for the client.

P1 shared,

> When I cannot help my clients, I feel like
> a lot of times they come in when they
> have experienced a domestic violence
> situation, and the woman and the
> children are trying to escape from their
> abuser ... leaving their own home,
> leaving all their belongings behind, and
> really, having nothing because they had

to leave everything just to get away and
they are left out on the street. They are
left in shelters, and even if they are in
shelters, they really do not have any of
their own stuff, and I go home … I think
about how the kids are impacted, and
how they do not have anything, and I
wonder what they are doing while I am
going home to my own house and my
own family and my own kids. I kind of
feel a sense of guilt on the way home.

P10 mentioned,

Honestly, I cannot function after. I
literally cannot function. I go home, and
I have to pick up my children after work.
Just the drive over there I am still trying
to alleviate the symptoms I am feeling
throughout the day. If I feel defeated or
I am upset, or if my chest hurts if I am a
little dizzy. I have not been able to
disconnect from the workday yet and by
the time I go pick up the kids and the

kids are full of energy. Because my job
has drained me, so it is affecting my
marriage. It is affecting my home
environment because I cannot, [I]
cannot, [I] cannot function. The only
time I get to function is on a Saturday
where I go to sleep on Friday night and
wake up and I am like 'okay.' I am not in
this environment and go on with the
routine. I am not coping very well.

P11 noted,

I can talk to a co-worker about it. I have
one specific co-worker that we kind of
vibe off each other. She will tell me her
things. I tell her mine. And that is kind
of our way of letting it out. After work,
we will discuss whatever case is
stressing us that day. Of having to
reach out to other providers and being
told to do this, do that. You do what
they say, and then you are told, 'You did
not do it right. You've got to do that or

that.' And then they tell you, 'We cannot provide for you what was originally told that we could provide.' I can relate with that because it is a lot of footwork to get the service you need, and then you do not end up getting it.

P12 mentioned,

> Well, for me, when they call me and I have just seen that client, we left everything was calm, and I get a call that, for example, my client is cutting herself and she is bleeding and there is yelling all over the place, and for me that is stressful, that I cannot do anything because I am not there, and trying to calm that person. I get very anxious, I get very … my anxiety level goes really high when I have to deal with these situations, especially when I am already home, and I really cannot go back and do anything, but try to guide them to either call 911. And, just try to help that

mother to deal with her child. Maybe because I am a mother, also. That has been very difficult to deal with, I think about it all the time.

P6 stated,

I do not think the day ever ends. I know that is bad because then you never get a break from it, but I do not know. I feel like whenever I have been in a role to do direct service it does not shut off because I am done with the client. I am still thinking about them. I am still thinking about how I am going to help. I am still thinking of resources. I am still thinking of approaches. I am still thinking. I am just always thinking about my clients and it just does not leave. I know it is not good, but at the end of the day, at the end of the workday, I go to the next thing. I am rushing to go pick up my son, but I am trying to engage with my son, but I am thinking about

how I am going to help this family. It
does not actually turn off until I actually
lay my head down and I actually get the
sleep that I need to put my mind to rest.

P3 shared,

My experience, I do get that often. You
go home and cannot get the client out of
your mind and you cannot stop thinking
about him/her, you know thinking how
that client is sleeping, how that client is
coping with whatever is going on with
his life so sometimes I ruminate, lack
sleep, overthink, and worry too much. I
do get that often. I do bring the client
home. I think about it a lot.

Core Theme 4: Self-Care Factors

Core theme 4 answers questions 7, 8, 9, and
10 (Appendix) as the patterns and themes came up.
Researchers have suggested there is a need for self-
care; however, there are only a small number of

studies that demonstrate how this can be conducted. This has been a concern, as researchers have suggested there are factors that affect practicing professionals in ways that make consideration to self-care and continuous wellness approaches crucial for proper and effective service provision (Baker, 2003a; Barnett et al., 2007; Dattilio, 2015; Goodwin & Richards, 2017; Wise et al., 2012). Self-care factors shared included how to incorporate self-care, the meaning of self-care, organizational support of self-care and support systems available.

P4 shared,

> Self-care is everything. Sometimes I do not know how to breathe. Sometimes I get so worked up just acknowledging that I can breathe is self-care. Self-care is investing in yourself the proper tender love and care to be able to give to others. You cannot give others what you do not have. Self-care is knowing yourself enough and using your experience to help, save, or show some

love to others. Life is about giving, and
self-care helps that. Self-care is all
about me.

P11 shared,

> It should mean more. I do not
> administer self-care. I can admit that. I
> just keep going. But self-care does
> mean to me ... if I used it ... taking care
> of myself and putting myself first. And
> make sure before I do anything that I am
> okay.

P1 shared,

> Self-care, for me, means taking care of
> myself. While most of my time, I am
> thinking about my clients and putting
> others first, I know that I cannot be a
> helpful or effective person if I cannot
> care for myself first, and that is what I
> stress to my clients, so to practice self-
> care means taking care of my physical

health and my emotional health and
meeting my own personal needs.

Sub-theme 4a: Self-care defined. Self-care
is defined as a complex, multifaceted progression of
intensive engagement of approaches that lead to
overall wellness (Dorociak et al., 2017). These
strategies and approaches endorse healthy
functioning and enhance well-being through activities
such as searching for personal therapy, enjoying
interpersonal relationships, creating change in the
workday, and participating in fun activities (Dorociak
et al., 2017). Although the term self-care has been
promoted, its meaning has not been fully explored in
the field of mental health and social work (Cox &
Steiner, 2013). Question 8 (Appendix) allowed the
participants to share their definition of self-care. All
12 mental-health workers responded, and their
definitions of self-care varied tremendously, from
going for walks to massages to more sleep. These
are the highlights.

P12 shared,

> Self-care means to me … going to get
> my nails done, going to get my feet
> done, going to get a massage, going to
> dinner with my family because they are
> the ones that are there for me. And it is
> very relaxing for me when I go out. And
> just being with my family helps me a lot,
> especially my [child]. My [child] and I
> are close. My [child] knows when I
> come home, stressed, and goes, 'Mom,
> you had a bad day.' And [my child] will
> go and make dinner, or [my child] will
> make plans to go out, so that is a
> wonderful thing. And my husband is
> supportive, and when he sees me
> stressed-out, he says, 'No. We're going
> out now.' We go dancing, I love going
> dancing.

P2 stated,

> Self-care. My time. So, self-care, to

me, is very simple. Self-care, to me, is
doing whatever it is that helps you feel
renewed and refreshed. Okay? So, for
me, people may think it is very, very
complicated. It's not. I can go to [chain
book store], where it is quiet. And, I can
look at magazines, have coffee … and I
love that. I am kind of an introvert, so
quiet activities are fantastic. Self-care
for me, I love photography, so I take
pictures of the moon.

P5 shared,

This is so huge. Self-care is just
humongous for me. I talk about it all the
time. I do not think … a week that does
not go by that I don't talk about self-
care. For me, self-care, my co-workers
laugh at me because I am a girly girl. I
am at the hairdresser. I go to the
hairdresser. I get out of work. Oh, I am
going to get my nails done. They are
like … you really take care of yourself. I

am … I have to, because my heart is so
big and being in this field when your
heart is big, you can be taken
advantage of. I am learning now
balance because the type of clients we
work with, they will keep taking, taking,
taking. Me, as a therapist, I, definitely
have balance but still, have my big
heart. I am able to do the job the way I
am, the way I do because I make sure I
do self-care weekly for myself, whether
it is going to take a walk in the park or
going to get my nails done or going to
hang out with one of my girlfriends and
have brunch, I make sure once a week I
do something for me. Yeah.

P6 noted,

It means I should be doing it. Self-care
is anything that helps us to just revive to
get re-boosted when we are
experiencing things, or we notice things
bothering us where it could lead to burn-

out. So, it is just basically those two words, taking care of yourself so you can be okay. Self-care for me comes in the form of connecting with nature like meditation, which I wish I was doing more often. Being outdoors, enjoying the seasons outside, which I try to do as much as possible, but I do not always have time. And, doing fun things but I do not always have the time to do it.

Sub-theme 4b: Workplace support of self-care. To provide beneficial treatment to clients, workers need to be mentally and physically healthy. Self-care needs to be implemented in work settings. According to Dorociak et al. (2017) when workers are healthy, outcomes are positive; preliminary studies which indicate self-care is related to professional well-being and outcomes (Dorociak et al., 2017). Social workers hold high regard to service provision, and it is instilled in every worker that clients are first; the code of ethics states a worker's primary goal is to assist people in need, advocate for social issues, and provide service to others above self-regard (NASW,

2017; Wheeler & McClain, 2015). There is not enough concern expressed for the emotional and physical care of the worker. Question 10 (Appendix) allowed the participants to describe and share the ways in which their place of work supported self-care. All of the mental-health workers described workplace support of self-care.

P1 shared,

> Everyone kind of gives an idea of what they do for self-care. It is something we occasionally touch on. I do not know if we do it as much as we should, because we are all mental-health workers and all of us are slammed with caseloads and notes and our schedules are packed back to back-to-back every single day, so it does not give us a lot of time, and we do not have the time to care for ourselves like we should. I do not think we actually touch on that part as much as we should, especially when we are trying to promote this to our clients,

when we ourselves are not able to do it
ourselves … we need to figure out a
way to schedule in time we are able to
take little breaks in the day or to be able
to care for ourselves more.

P10 shared,

> I would love for it to be about my self-
> care at any given moment I am able to
> do it physically do it. Right now, what I
> have gotten so far for promoting self-
> care would be that at the moment, that I
> am 'screaming' … I am drowning and I
> am feeling stressed. I said screaming
> because I could, I am a very vocal
> person. I can vocalize it. I can … it is
> very evident because I am a very
> expressive person. I am feeling it. They
> are ignoring it because the work is
> getting done. Yes, you are stressed out,
> but we have what we need. Someone
> needs to stress, and it is you, right. They
> ignore the fact so when I scream it out,

like listen, this is what is going on. I need help. I have to really scream it because being vocal and professional isn't sufficient. Being expressive about it, which is evident. Now that I tend to be expressive is not enough and I had to scream it out. Then I get well you know what, maybe you need a day off. I am like okay. Everybody loves a day off. I take that day off and I come back with nothing being done and the day that I do come back it is worse than the day before that I took the day off. The day before I take off to enjoy my next day, I am doing a thousand and one things in hopes when I do come back the following day, I do not have to have a stress day. It is not self-care. We do not have that accessibility, so we have clients coming in and out. What am I going to do just go on my break with a client just sitting there and I am staring? That is not taking a break. That is not self-care.

P11 shared,

I do not think they support self-care. I just do not. My suggestions would be to really sit down and speak with your staff. I feel like the workers, they do not care about their happiness or joy. And my life is not just work. I have a personal life like everybody here. I do not think there is a care we are human. It is just money, money, money, money, money. The result is the high turnover rate. If you do not have a staff that is happy or content … and that waiver. We are all human. Sometimes you have just got to do things. If you do not have staff that are happy about coming to work and whatever they are dealing with at home might be stressful and then you come, and you stress yourself out at work, something has got to go.

P12 mentioned,

> I do not think we have a lot of self-care
> activities at our job. Once in a while, we
> will have someone come in and they will
> talk about self-care, but we have not
> had it in a long time. We used to have
> team building and they would really
> listen to what is going on with us.
> Recently we have not had a lot of self-
> care activities. And that is my opinion.

P2 mentioned,

> We are in a very busy place. I think
> that, in any health-care industry, we
> focus on care for the patients, and care
> for the clients, and care for the families,
> but we don't … we do not really do it to
> us, to ourselves. We do not look at
> ourselves as people who also need
> care. Right now we have a Biggest
> Loser thing. And it is focused on weight
> loss, and everybody participates. And …

it gives us the opportunity to eat better, eat healthier. And from time-to-time, they have like walks ... so those are things. But again, do we have the time? There is not really a set, carved time where it says, okay, the world will stop here in the agency now, between 12:00 and 12:20, and we are going to do this specific self-care gear activity, and everybody is going to participate. They have tried to implement some things during the staff meetings. They brought people in, someone that does reiki. I don't know if that is encompassing, really, self-care for everybody, right? I think they have tried. I do not know that you know, how busy it is, it is really something promoted all the time, or practiced all the time. We do promote it. We will say oh, take care of yourself. You know, do something good for yourself. But not really, you know, here, at the workplace.

Sub-theme 4c: Activities to engage in self-care. It is of importance to identify self-care strategies in addition to trauma training. The significance of self-care in mental-health workers is documented; however, there is not enough information concerning specific ways in which the helpers manage stress when faced with clients suffering or experiencing trauma. (Cox & Steiner, 2013). Question 9 (Appendix) opened a significant platform in which participants shared methods with which they practice self-care. The mental-health workers identified personal activities related to self-care such as spending time with family, sleeping, hobbies, walks in the park, and dancing.

P1 shared,

> When I leave work, I try to put a barrier
> between everything I have done during
> the day, because I do not want to take
> my anxiety and stress of working with
> high trauma clients home with me; I try
> to separate work and my home life as
> much as I can, because I am also on

call a lot. When I leave here, I turn on music. I am a dancer, and I like to put on my playlist, and I like to choreograph dances in my head, and that makes me focus on the steps, and sometimes I will hear the song a different day and I will add to the dance in my head, but what it is doing is allowing me to put focus on my present and kind of leaving work behind as I drive away, and that puts the barrier up. When I get home, I am able to focus on my family and my kids and my home life, and I am already past work. I also spend time with my kids. We go to the park. I like to exercise. I try to exercise every single day, but I think now, in today's society, because we have so many roles, it is really hard to really practice self-care the way we should or the way we want to, so I feel like as much stress and stuff I have experienced at work, it is really, there is not enough time to really do the self-care that I need.

P10 shared,

> What I do right now as I mentioned I do
> have my business. It started out as a
> hobby and then became an actual full-
> blown business and it builds momentum
> very quickly, and it was not something I
> was expecting. I am just ... I am going
> to take this ride wherever this business
> takes me. Which is a beautiful thing? I
> think that would be more of a self-care if
> I was able to do it during the week and
> be able to expand it. That was
> supposed to be my initial self-care. That
> was something I got into my husband
> says maybe you should do something
> outside of the home for you, that you are
> away from the kids because I know you
> are having a hard time with work and
> everything, that is yours. It is your own
> thing. No one is going to take that away
> from you. It is your own time, your own
> space, your own everything. So that is
> my biggest self-care on a Saturday.

P11 shared,

More sleep. Sleeping in on Saturday.
Going to the gym. That I drifted away
from, but now coming back. Going to
church. Every Sunday, that has been
the one consistent thing that I can do for
myself as self-care. It is kind of like my
re-set button. That is about it so far.

P12 shared,

Dancing. I love dancing. We have a lot
of family functions. My family's large.
We have a lot of celebrations, almost
every month. Birthdays, we have
anniversaries. My sister-in-law, she has
parties for women, just women, and
everybody brings a dish and we switch
gifts. It is very nice to go and be with
your family and friends.

P2 mentioned,

> It is going to the park and waiting for the
> moon to come out. I love it. You know,
> and it is what, five minutes, ten minutes
> between you know, the moon rising up
> to the sky. So, there are little things that
> I like to do. And then brainless activities
> sometimes are self-care, because they
> bring me out, they take me out of that
> mode. The photography, because I am
> there, and when I am there it is just me
> in the park. It allows me to just be
> present, right? Look at the birds, look at
> the sunset going on behind me, looking
> at nature and just breathing, some
> different air because you are kind of in a
> park with a lot of trees. It is a different
> place. Going to the park, again, it is the
> solitude of maybe just having that walk
> by yourself, and trying not to think of
> anything but feeling, maybe … your
> steps going. Just being present and
> looking at the water and the details of

the water. Those are things that help me, I think. My nails. I may go for my nails, for my hair. I may say, okay let me go and have my hair done, or have my ... have a pedicure. And again, what I love the most about the pedicure is not really the nail color. Sometimes I do not even pick the nail color. It is the massage chair and sitting there and just closing my eyes and not having to do or think about anything. Those are activities I do.

Sub-theme 4d: Support systems available. Stress, lack of self-care, the absence of a culture of care and support systems within a working organization can be detrimental to the helping profession and the social work profession. Coordination and response from researchers, policymakers, and agency leaders are needed to address these issues; without this, professionals are left susceptible to the shared burden of trauma accrued from chronic and acute adversity, which is also known as VT and STS (Molnar et al., 2017).

Question number 7 (Appendix), allowed participants to share their thoughts on the support systems at work available to them. The identified support systems included supervision and peer support.

P6 noted,

> My supervisor. My supervisor and my co-workers. My supervisor always tells me that I can always call, but you know if it is late at night I am not going to call my supervisor so. That is just ... I don't know. I feel like my co-workers have been a great support because we are in the office together and we talk. We talk about cases. We talk about life. We talk about everything. It is easier, so that is where I bring my anxiety and my stress for sure, because they understand. They are not going to judge and if they see something or hear something, they are going to tell me. Like well, what? Or have you tried, or they are going to probe.

P7 noted,

> Believe it or not, we are surrounded by clinicians, and I feel like I do not have anybody. I mean, we are told it is an open-door policy. If you are feeling anything we can go and speak on it. I just do not … our days are so fast that you, kind of do not take a moment to stop and go speak to someone in regard to; anything trauma related or that you are hearing from a client. If it is not work-related, you push it to the side and continue working on your daily duties. A support system would be your supervisor we can go to. If we are talking about work, supervisors are always there. The CEO is always there. It is an open-door policy, whether we decide to use it or not, do we find the time to use it during our work schedule, then that is a different story.

P8 noted,

> Oh, my team is wonderful, my
> supervisor is wonderful. And at any
> moment I can grab anybody. I can grab
> anyone, and debrief and process. And
> through the years I have learned, I
> cannot keep it here. Like, on my chest.
> Whatever has been unloaded onto me,
> from a client, I need to release that. I
> need to let that out. That goes back to
> me talking about it. Because then that
> can help bring down my stress, and my
> anxiety. And help me move forward
> better. That emotion, when you are
> sitting there, and you are being there
> with a client, and you are relating to the
> client ... they are giving you everything
> they have been through ... everything
> they are feeling right now. You kind of
> have to get into their shoes to
> understand them, and relate, and
> validate, and support. Holding that
> feeling is hard. When it is not yours.

And it is not your problems, it is really
hard. And so how do I release that?
And I have learned through the years,
my team, people that I can debrief with,
and talk about the case. And just listen.
You do not have to brainstorm my case,
just listen. And it works.

P9 mentioned,

We have supervision. We can talk
about it with the supervisor, and also,
we have ... we can take the time and
speak with our co-workers like, how I
feel about this situation. How I feel
about this client and just talk to
someone and just do not stop it and go
home with that.

**Sub-theme 4e: Suggestions to improve
activities.** This next theme was developed from
participants' responses to open suggestions for
improving activities that would incorporate self-care
within their organization; it is the second part of

question 10 (Appendix). All 12 mental-health workers suggested improvements of self-care activities, such as having open discussions concerning needs, bringing in speakers, having management check in with workers, and activities such as massages for the workers.

P1 mentioned,

> I think that we should, as an agency …
> have a bigger discussion about it,
> whereas we just touch on it and go
> around the room, and everyone says
> what is self-care, and it kind of sounds
> like a book definition when we talk about
> it. I think that, even if people are afraid
> to speak up, what they really need from
> the agency, I think maybe we could do a
> survey. Something that will allow
> everyone to voice what they're feeling,
> rather than putting them on the spot in a
> group situation. A lot of times, I think we
> hold back when it is our CEO running a
> meeting, and no one wants to really say

what they are really feeling. I think they are fearful. This is their job, and this is the way it is, so a lot of people see their job like this is what is defined, and this is my role; we have to meet our numbers and we have to get productivity, so we do not really have a say. If everyone was able to really voice what they really wanted, as far as maybe doing things more as an agency together and becoming more cohesive, and all of the programs are a little bit separated, it could be a benefit for the entire program and the entire agency.

P10 stated,

I really think what will eliminate some of the stress and anxiety would be if people start opening up their eyes. Start off there. Or open up their eyes and start acknowledging the fact that is what I am stating. Acknowledging the fact of what is really going on, so they could figure out a way to alleviate. But right now, they are cognizant of it, but they do not want to be ... they are aware of it, but they do not want to do action in regard to alleviate everyone's stress. I would like it to start there. Figure out how you are going to do self-care. How? How can you help me with self-care? This agency does not. Well, what I have seen does not provide it. I really would like ... it would have been nice that we have ... agency retreats. Agency retreats or its Christmas time let us have an agency Christmas party or an annual staff appreciation day. Or let us just stop, even if it is just for a couple of minutes, I am not expecting to close on the agency and lose revenue but maybe take a day to do massages or actually a self-care convention like massages and ways to cope with stresses or exercise, team building or anything that is like, even if they're okay one day we are going to take you out and everyone is going to go and everyone is going to paint their nails with someone that is coming in. I want to do that.

P11 mentioned,

I wish self-care was more promoted … it is like said out the mouth, but not actually put in place. How can we actually initiate this if we are not shown it? If it is really not promoted seriously, it is just one of the things like, 'Yeah, you will figure it out. Go ahead and do it.' If we are not shown it and we feel as though they do not care ... and by not caring it is like more work on top of more. We know what is got to get done, and sometimes there is going to be stressful times. That is just the nature of anybody's job. The way they go about it, it is like I know there is not a care. It is like as long as we make the numbers … as long as the notes are in, so they can get paid. They are not really looking at it because if you saw how some people looked if you just took the time to look at people, you would see by their affect that they are not well. I do not think upper management, management pays enough attention to slow someone down and say, 'Hey, what's wrong? Are you okay?' Well, if they regularly come in and you are used to a certain look about them, and they are coming in and they are not maybe dressed the same way, their face is not the same way, they look sad or maybe they are not giving as much conversation as they used to, they are not doing that…

P12 mentioned,

Yes, I have suggestions. I think they should have … the team building, that should come back. I think they should have, I know we could have massages, where massage students could come in, and we used to do that. They could come in and do massages. Those are the things that, if they could do that, that is very relaxing. I feel if we do all that within the agency, I think people would, I think they would be better or be more relaxed and feel supported.

Reflective Journal Data

A reflective journal was started at the commencement of the project and continued through data collection. Entries were made after each interview where reflections and thoughts were documented. A content analysis of the journal entries demonstrates parallel reactions to the experiences the participants shared. These reactions manifested as similar symptoms of VT/STS. There were times when the researcher experienced (when working with) victims of trauma. The content analysis reflected physical, emotional, and empathic reactions. Several participants highlighted the effects and symptoms associated with VT. These are some journal entries.

June 1, 2018. P1 openly shared how she was abused as a child sexually and physically and as an adult as well and lived with domestic violence. P1 shared how she could relate to many of her cases as she had experienced the trauma herself. P1 cried openly, but was able to continue without interruptions. As the interview progressed, she became more comfortable. P1 shared she experiences nightmares, heart palpitations, and stabbing pains at times as a physical sign of work-related stress. P1 shared how she feels self-care is important and how she tries to practice this as she dances and spends time with her children. P1 shared she would like more self-care collectively at the organization, as it is not taken seriously. She stated she uses supervision and this is effective, she also uses peer support. She feels the organization can improve on this. (The researcher felt bad that she cried as she remembered the cases she worked with and as she shared that she had been a victim of abuse, and she shared how she had personal trauma in her life). The researcher provided a period of debriefing after the interview.

June 1, 2018. P8 appeared quiet, however confident. P8 shared how stressful work is to her, however, every day is hard as she does not know what she will face. P8 shared stories the clients shared are very stressful for her, and it takes her back to her own personal traumatic and domestic violent experiences. She was very open and honest and teared up as she spoke. (This made the researcher emotional as well … close to tears as the participant disclosed a very personal traumatic experience with a client.) She shared how she accompanied a young client to

an abortion clinic after a rape. P8
shared she cried for days after this. P8
stated she experiences lots of anxiety
and her feet shake at times. She uses
supervision and her peers as a support
system. P8 states she works hard to
stay away from traumatic work and
thoughts that led to feelings of
depression. She states the cases stay
in her head and she tries to not think of
them by either reading or watching a
movie. She experienced the same
trauma as her young client, however
she feels it deeply. P8 cried openly and
the researcher asked if she wanted to
continue. She said yes. P8 stated her
organization does encourage mental-
health workers to use outside sources
for support if needed. P8 was provided
with a time to debrief afterward.

June 22, 2018. P12 came in on time,
she was nervous. After the researcher
normalized and explained the process

she was more comfortable. P12 has a very long history working in the field and has shared many different roles. She also added more, after debriefing, as she stated she was quite nervous and left some things out. As with the other participants, the researcher was compelled to hug her, however, the researcher had to remind self of research role and not as a therapist, even though emotional at times. The researcher was wondering could this too be called vicarious trauma? Talking about trauma and its effects on the mental health worker. Feelings of sadness and tears were hard to hold back. The researcher saw working with individuals and hearing their stories and being part of their lives, is difficult and the boundaries mental-health professionals were taught to follow, disintegrate as they are swept into the stories of pain and even torture … that some of these individuals have

experienced at work and in their
personal lives. The researcher put bias
on the side and bracketed ... P12 was
provided with time to debrief as well as
informed of the process of member
checking.

Summary

The presentation of these results demonstrates
a description of 12 mental-health workers' lived
experiences of coping with VT/STS and how they use
self-care in coping with trauma. Overall, the mental-
health workers shared similar experiences, as evident
by the patterns and themes reflected in their
interviews. The qualitative methodology, and the
phenomenological approach employed, allowed the
mental-health workers to share aspects of daily
exposure to trauma work. Utilizing the interview guide
as a tool, participants were encouraged to discuss
aspects of their lived experiences in the field, starting
with their experiences at work, to the level of agency
support, activities to engage in self-care, and
recommendations on improving these activities.

All of the participants were able to engage,
answer the questions, and establish rapport easily
with the researcher. Interviews were completed in
their entirety with no breaks and no issues.
Participants were provided with a period of debriefing
upon completion of the interview. Post-interview,
member-checking validated contents, with minimal
corrections needed, and were mostly grammatical
corrections. The researcher's journal provided data
used to explore and validate the participants'
experiences. In addition to the research data results,
what stands out is the love participants have for the
profession and the dedication they demonstrate in
their jobs, even though they face tough situations
daily. The participants in the study's ability to manage
their professional lives, work, and feelings are
admirable. The mental-health provider participants
had the capability to see their situation and that of
their clients and colleagues, through numerous
perspectives, stemming from hope to frustration to
despair and back to hope, and never forgetting who
they were and what their work means to them. This
was evidence of true career commitment. The
discussion that follows draws conclusions and sets

recommendations based on the outcomes of the
present investigation.

Chapter 5

Results, Conclusions,
and Recommendations

Introduction

The purpose of this research study was to investigate mental-health workers' lived experiences of coping with VT and how they practice self-care. To present an effective dialog between mental-health workers, VT, and self-care, a strong foundation must be established. This foundation has been established through a transition from the research questions, previous research, methodologies for the study, to data collection, and findings. Using a transcendental phenomenological approach, 12 mental-health workers employed at a community clinic from a northeastern state were interviewed to capture their lived experiences of coping with VT, and how they practice self-care.

Summary of the Results

Data was gathered from demographic paper surveys, semi-structured interviews, and a reflective journal. Post-interview member checking provided validity and additional data confirmed the findings. The reflective journal produced a triangulation of data and documentation which also served as affirmations. The findings of this qualitative phenomenological study demonstrate patterns and themes that provide a direct link related to the effects that VT has on mental-health workers. Participants shared work-related feelings and thoughts, as well as physical symptoms associated with work, stress, and anxiety. The identified patterns and themes captured from the rich descriptions demonstrate different areas of the mental-health workers' schema that have been affected, as described by their 'lived experiences.' These experiences were captured and labeled into four core themes: workplace factors, interactions with clients, stress factors, and self-care. In addition, 12 sub-themes were also identified.

The research question that guided this study was, "How do mental-health workers describe coping with vicarious trauma?" The research sub-question was, "How do mental-health workers use self-care in response to vicarious trauma?"

The study yielded results that answered the research question and the sub-question. From the descriptions of the lived experience shared by the workers, it was discovered mental-health workers have few coping strategies to effectively manage VT. All 12 of the mental-health workers had their own personal meaning of self-care; therefore, they adapted self-care techniques derived from these personal definitions and interpretations. Mental-health workers who did practice self-care did not do so daily, nor did they have a standard of self-care related to managing VT.

There is a need to explore this area as the welfare of mental-health professionals directly impacts service provision (Molnar et al., 2017). While at work, practitioners are exposed to a huge amount of experiences shared by their patients (Halevi & Idisis, 2017). As a result, workers are experiencing significant reactions. These reactions may be observed by an alteration in expressive, cognitive, and physical behavior in the mental-health professionals that may be displayed as post-traumatic symptoms such as disturbing memories (flashbacks), hyperarousal, evasion of normal life situations, increase in personal issues, and a decrease in the enjoyment of everyday life (Halevi & Idisis, 2017). The constructivist self-development theory, adapted as the framework for this study as the basic tenants of the CSDT, are that people have the intrinsic capability of constructing their own realisms as they interrelate with environments (McCann & Pearlman, 1990a).

The constructivist self-development theory, applied specifically to the trauma worker, points to ways in which working with trauma victims can disturb a counselor's imagery system of recollection, as well as schema about the self and others (Dunkley & Whelan, 2006; McCann & Pearlman, 1993). The response to trauma is a complex process that includes an individual's meaning and images of events extending to the most profound parts of a person's experience of themselves and the world, resulting in unique changes (McCann & Pearlman, 1990a).

Previous research demonstrates the personal and professional damage that VT and STS can cause a mental health worker; studies have demonstrated that service provision is affected when the worker has become affected by either VT or STS (Dorociak et al., 2017; Knight, 2013; Sansbury et al., 2015). The literature review documented the consequences of vicarious traumatization – long term effects on mental-health workers.

Discussion of the Results

The first research question guiding this study was, "How do mental-health workers describe coping with vicarious trauma?" The participants voiced experience of anxiety and stress, feelings of inadequacy, recurring thoughts, physical symptoms, and identification with client issues when coping with VT. The data analysis showed common themes related to these feelings. The mental-health workers described their work experience as intense, demanding, stressful, draining, hard, frustrating, difficult, and challenging. Mental-health workers shared that administrative demands and deadlines added to feelings associated with anxiety and stress.

Despite their anxieties and stress, mental-health workers continue to work. They described the love they have for their work regardless of these feelings. Mental-health professionals continue to provide services regardless of the emotional and physical feelings they are experiencing. Due to the awareness that caring for traumatized individuals comes at a cost for the mental-health workers in the field, there has been growing research interest in the emotional repercussions of caring for individuals who have had distressing experiences and the way in which it affects the helping professional (Hyatt-Burkhart, 2014). The results of this study demonstrated that mental-health workers are dedicated professionals who put their own feelings and needs aside to serve their clients. At the clinical level, Hernandez Wolfe et al. (2015) found addressing VT within education, training, and offering cognitive understanding by a focused supervision would prevent burnout and instill a sense of optimism for the therapist.

The mental-health workers shared feelings of inadequacy as they provide services, at times feeling that they needed more support, supervision, or

training. Through exposure to clients' revelations and

sharing of traumatic experiences, mental-health

workers and others in the helping professions become

at risk of effects and symptoms caused by VT/STS;

depression, anxiety, intrusive imagery, numbing,

avoidance phenomena, cognitive shifts, and social,

professional, and personal problems are a few

(Cetrano et al., 2017). The mental-health workers in

this study, while dedicated to their work, experienced

feelings of uncertainty as they questioned their own

professionalism, knowledge, and judgment, which is

indicative of a shift in cognition. Providing additional

supervision would be beneficial; however, the workers

would not always seek supervision for fear that doing

so would be seen as them admitting to being unable

to perform their job.

Workers shared identifying with client issues

due to personal past trauma. When workers are

vicariously traumatized, having experienced similar

past trauma may affect service provision. Although

workers shared an identification with client issues,

none of the workers mentioned receiving outside help,

despite being clearly affected by such identification.

Both STS and VT can play an undesirable role in service provision. Symptoms of STS can impact healthcare professionals and the treatment they deliver. Mental-health workers and other professionals may be at higher risk of having a poor professional judgment, which may negatively impact diagnosis and treatment planning (Kintzle et al., 2013). Pearlman and Maclan (1995) found workers who had been traumatized previously had higher chances of developing VT due to heightened susceptibility. The mental-health workers expressed feelings of identifying with clients; they did not feel it was appropriate to share this information with a supervisor (as it was 'personal'). None of the workers disclosed any attempts to obtain outside help or other ways of coping with these feelings.

In addition to identifying with client issues, two workers expressed they relived client sessions through documentation … another stress factor. Previous research from the literature review did not identify this issue. One participant disclosed the same feelings of reliving the client trauma while documenting her notes while debriefing, as she stated she forgot to mention this. This addendum added to the results of this study by indicating that, not only do the mental-health workers relive their own experiences through the accounts of the stories shared by their traumatized clients, but they also relive it again while documenting the day's notes.

Although the workers identified anxiety and stress related to working directly with traumatized individuals, the mental-health professionals added that administrative demands add to the stress and anxiety already built up; they do not feel as if the agency or the organization understands the amount of stress or anxiety that is experienced. The mental-health workers shared a common theme where they felt the organization does not realize administrative responsibilities, with which they are encumbered, adds to their stress and anxiety. Vicarious trauma and STS can disrupt a professional and the service they provide; therefore, studying ways in which organizations can provide support would benefit the worker, the client, and the organization. It would benefit mental-health workers if supervising management was educated on the effects VT/STS may have on a worker and to provide additional support and training. According to Choi (2011),

administrators, supervising managers, and
administrative leaders, who provide more access to
organizational strategic information, can prevent STS
among their staff.

All 12 mental-health workers described
experiencing physical symptoms related to stress and
anxiety related to work. Data analysis showed
common themes of stress, anxiety, feelings of
inadequacy, recurring thoughts, sleeplessness,
nightmares, hyper-vigilance, heart palpitations, panic,
breathing difficulty, migraines, headaches, and
appetite issues. Although all 12 mental-health
workers shared physical symptoms associated with
work, not one worker stated seeking medical attention
due to these symptoms nor did they mention calling
out due to feeling ill. Studies continue to demonstrate
the effects of VT/STS on the helping professional
(Caringi et al., 2017; Connally, 2012; Shannonhouse
et al., 2016); however, the researchers failed to
identify any treatment. This study demonstrates how
VT and STS affect the working professionals who
work with trauma. The mental-health workers
described physical symptoms with both professional
and personal affects. The mental-health workers

described how these symptoms are with them, not only during work hours, but after they leave work. While the helping workers do attribute the physical symptoms to work, they did not identify ways to treat them.

Almost all of the mental-health workers shared recurring thoughts related to work after their day of work had ended. The thoughts interfered with their lives even after work. The mental-health workers described work experiences so intense, they had difficulty 'escaping.' Vicarious trauma causes a powerful transformation on the therapist's inner world, inclusive of schemas, beliefs, and values, leading to lasting psychological and emotional variation (McCormack & Adams, 2016; Pearlman & Saakvitne, 1995).

The research sub-question that guided the study was, "How do mental-health workers use self-care in response to vicarious trauma?" The mental-health workers all had their own definition of self-care. While some practiced some type of self-care, all of them practiced strategies they developed from their own interpretations of self-care. None of the mental-health workers followed an identified curriculum or any type of organizational program. Self-care is demarcated as a complex, process of purposeful engagement of strategies that mark the path to increased wellness (Dorociak et al., 2017). These strategies improve healthy functioning and boost well-being through personal therapy, taking time for personal relationships, creating change in the workday, and participating in funfilled activities (Dorociak et al., 2017).

As research outcomes demonstrate that VT and STS can affect individuals regardless of age or gender, job title, or work environment, if there is interaction with a traumatized client, there will be a risk of VT and STS. Not all therapists will be vicariously traumatized. While researchers continue rigorous studies on the phenomenon, it would benefit mental health providers to practice self-care in addition to other supports. Best practices in health and mental health care begin with self-care (Goodwin & Richards, 2017). All of the mental-health workers defined self-care as they personally understood it. The mental-health workers shared ways they practiced self-care, including getting their nails and hair done, getting a massage, spending time with family, dancing, photography, reading, going to church, cooking, and sleeping. Although they made time for these activities, the activities were unrelated to work.

Almost all the mental-health workers felt the organization for whom they worked lacks self-care support. Although the term self-care has recently been promoted in the field, its meaning has not been fully explored in the field of mental-health research (Cox & Steiner, 2013). It would benefit organizations and the field of social work if attention was brought to this issue.

Some research writers have recognized an imperative for professionals to incorporate self-care approaches that fall into two important categories of lifestyle or workplace modifications (Cox & Steiner, 2013; Norcross & Guy, 2007). While mental-health workers encourage clients to practice self-care, many do not practice it themselves. Baker (2003b) stated, "the process of becoming attuned to and responsible for one's self is, in fact, developmental" (p. 25).

While these suggestions are all accepted, it is important to mention the needs of therapists increase and may change as they evolve as practitioners and

are supported in different ways. While some workers
may need more supervision, others may need more
administrative time, organizational support, or
customized support. Customized support refers to
offering support tailored to the need, e.g., while
therapist A may need more supervision, therapist B
may need an outside referral to additional
professional help.

While the mental-health workers shared
activities to engage in self-care, and their favorite
ways of engaging in self-care, they did not describe
self-care as a priority. For example, while P7 shared
that she is too tired to practice self-care, P9 shared
that she enjoys time with her family. As stated
previously, mental-health workers are exhausted from
work, often times taking the work home with them
through recurring thoughts, which may lead to
increased anxiety and stress.

Baker (2003a), points out, "learning to pay
attention to and be respectful of one's needs and to
meet them responsibly, is a lifelong task for the
therapist as well as for patients" (p. 60). It is
imperative mental-health workers, administrators, and
organizations identify the need for emotional and

physical self-care and make it a priority. Researchers suggested there are factors that interfere with practicing professionals in ways that make consideration to self-care and continued wellness efforts essential for ethical and comprehensive practice (Baker, 2003a; Barnett et al., 2007; Dattilio, 2015; Goodwin & Richards, 2017; Wise et al., 2012).

This research study's results also demonstrate – although the mental-health workers identify supervision as a support – the workers continue to experience these negative thoughts and feelings. According to Choi (2011), VT/STS is not a product of ineffective supervision. The mental-health workers shared they participated in supervision regularly and they had supervision available to them in times of crisis. P11 shared frustration with supervision and noted the inability to speak to a supervisor late at night. This may be indicative of specific needs of individual workers. As noted, this study's mental-health workers all practiced self-care in different ways, and each had different supports available.

The last sub-theme was suggestions to improve activities. There were a number of suggestions reflective of the themes. Suggestions included taking surveys, doing yoga, massages while at lunch, and participating in outside activities as a team. The mental-health workers experience physical and emotional distress at work and demonstrated an eagerness for change and teamwork from their interview responses.

While the mental-health workers shared their experiences at work and how they cope with VT, which included anxieties, stress, thoughts, physical symptoms identifying with clients, and self-care strategies, not one mental-health worker shared thoughts of leaving the job, disappointment with peers, or leaving the profession. The mental-health profession has instilled in every worker that clients are the priority, as noted in the profession's code of ethics. The social worker's primary goals are to help people in need, address social problems, and elevate service to others above self-interest (Wheeler & McClain, 2015).

It would benefit organizations and educators to focus on mental-health workers, VT, and self-care as the helping profession would be at a loss without such professionals working in the field. There is a need to pay attention to subtle changes and behaviors which would be indicative of a worker under stress and in need of support. Mental-health professionals ignore their own mental health and health needs; thereby possibly affecting treatment they provide for clients.

Discussion of the Conclusions

The purpose of this qualitative study was to investigate mental-health workers' lived experiences of coping with VT and how they incorporate self-care. The research question that guided this study was, "How do mental-health workers describe coping with vicarious trauma?" The research sub-question was, "How do mental-health workers use self-care in response to vicarious trauma?" The research problem (theory) was mental-health workers who do experience VT seldom practice self-care.

The workers voiced being affected at different levels of stress. The levels may have to do with the length of time in the field, a personal history of trauma, or support systems or lack of. There is a disconnect between the self-care of workers who experience VT and the meaning of self-care. What is known is that working with trauma may affect helping professionals and those work-related effects can morph into their personal lives. Vicarious trauma and STS are significant occupational hazards for mental-health professionals; VT and STS could have negative effects on the quality of their personal and interpersonal associations (Branson et al., 2014).

The mental-health worker participants in this research study did not identify outside resources for support or any formal procedures which would lead to the treatment, management, or identification of VT or the practice of self-care. There were four core themes that emerged from the data analysis, as well as 12 additional sub-themes. The core themes were workplace factors, client interactions, stress factors, and self-care factors. The workers were able to share candidly how they coped with VT while they shared their lived experiences. The collective results indicate there is no specific coping strategy when dealing with VT/STS, even though the mental-health workers share various behaviors and feelings directly associated with being vicariously traumatized or experiencing STS.

The workers shared how they felt stress and anxiety related to work responsibilities. They described their work as intense, challenging, frustrating, and hard. The mental-health professional study participants also shared feelings of inadequacy and their inability to focus or provide appropriate treatment due to a lack of supervision and training. Physical symptoms associated with stress and anxiety at work were not addressed in or out of work. The workers shared that they often thought of work after the day was over. The workers also shared that, although they have supervision, supervision is not enough to support the feelings or behaviors associated with VT. One worker stated she often thought about work late at night and that recurring thoughts plagued her before bedtime, and she believed there was no one to which she could speak. According to Choi (2011), STS is not a consequence of insufficient supervision.

This study on the effects of VT on the overall daily experience adds to the body of knowledge by providing professionals in the field, educators, and mental health organizations an opportunity to examine the experiences of the individuals who are experiencing the phenomenon. The outcomes of this study will lead to tools for the helping professionals to manage daily experiences, which may have been caused internal turmoil or feelings of inadequacy.

Stress, lack of self-care, and the absence of a culture of care within an organization can be detrimental to the helping profession and the social work profession. Without a collective effort from researchers, politicians, and organizational leaders, these professionals are left susceptible to the shared burden of trauma accumulated from chronic and acute hardship, also known as VT and STS (Molnar et al., 2017).

The constructivist self-development theory was the framework for this investigation. McCann and Pearlman's (1990b) constructivist self-development theory (CSDT) delivers a comprehensive conceptual framework for grasping VT. When applied to the trauma therapist, the theory points out explicit ways in which working with distressed victims can disturb the counselor's system of recollection, as well as outlook about the self and others (Dunkley & Whelan, 2006; McCann & Pearlman, 1993). Using the CSDT as a framework for the study provided a clear understanding in answering the research questions and sub-questions. The findings of this study align with CSDT, as demonstrated by the mental-health workers' responses to the interview questions. The patterns and themes generated by the data analysis represent examples of distortions in imagery and disruptions of the mental-health workers' schema about the self and others. This can lead to changes in feelings and behaviors that can affect the workers personally and professionally.

Even though these mental-health professionals have been considered competent to work in these demanding situations, many of these workers are emotionally harmed by the distressing (sometimes traumatic) experiences of the families and/or individual clients they serve (Caringi et al., 2017). The outcomes of this study demonstrate a link between behavior and feelings caused by VT, which in turn affect the way the worker thinks or processes thoughts.

Previous studies demonstrated the effects of VT and how it affects the workers. Vicarious trauma has negative consequences on the provider; the symptoms almost mimic the symptoms being experienced by the victim. Vicarious trauma may affect the professional mental-health worker

depending on their own history of trauma, support
system, and individual differences. For example,
Hernandez-Wolfe et al. (2015) explored the
connection between vicarious traumatization and
vicarious resilience and looked at a possibility of co-
existence. Hernandez-Wolfe et al. (2015), conducted
a qualitative study to examine the coexistence of
vicarious resilience and VT in trauma work with
torture survivors in specialized programs across the
United States using a constructivist framework.
Similar to the Hernandez-Wolfe et al. (2015) study,
mental-health workers in this study presented as
resilient and loved their work, although they were
presenting with symptoms of STS. The mental-health
workers in this research study shared they felt content
when accomplishing work-related goals.

McCormack and Adams (2016) mentioned
that, without the right organizational support, a
therapist in a work setting may be in danger of poor
self-actualization. Therapists lacking organizational-
supervisory support may undergo long-lasting
psychopathology as they struggle to make sense of
their anguish from VT exposure (Hernandez-Wolfe et
al., 2015). Vicarious trauma may lead to a powerful

alteration on the therapist's inner world, inclusive of schemas, beliefs, and values, causing lasting psychological and emotional variations (McCormack & Adams, 2016; Pearlman & Saakvitne, 1995). The results of this study demonstrated that workers experiencing VT, are affecting them emotionally and physically; awareness needs to be bought on, which includes the management team, supervisors, and the organization as a whole. To promote wellness and provide support, the organization needs to be educated on the long-lasting consequences of VT and STS and trained on how to deal with worker's symptoms.

Caringi et al. (2017) concluded that agency-based, mental-health workers, especially those involved with stressful cases, are at jeopardy of acquiring STS; it is crucial to understand the organizational features that may impact vulnerable workers. Shannon et al. (2014) concluded in their study that comprehension in the way students become professionally acquainted with the practice of effective self-care may alternately contribute to the deterrence of VT and STS among social workers exposed to trauma in their work. An understanding of

VT and consequences associated with it may be effective in identifying, managing, and treating VT and STS. The mental-health workers in this research study were knowledgeable of VT; they felt now there was more awareness being highlighted for the phenomena.

Cox and Steiner (2013) conducted a participatory research study to explore the prevalence of vicarious traumatic stress in the social work field and strategies used to overcome or prevent VT. The researchers used the CSDT as a framework for their study. The findings demonstrated thinking patterns and themes associated with the strengths and abilities of social workers when managing a client's pain, suffering, and trauma. The researchers suggested social workers who have a history of trauma should seek out additional help, supervision should be readily available to trauma workers, and organizations should provide a culture-of-care to enable workers to process these experiences (Cox & Steiner, 2013). Most of the mental-health workers in this study shared having experienced trauma previously in their personal lives and that experience did play a role as they provided service to their clients. They did not share this previous experience with their supervisors or peers, nor did they receive outside help for this. The mental-health workers felt sharing this made them feel either inadequate at the job or it played a part in recurring thoughts. Cox and Steiner (2013) suggest a therapist should seek outside help and the organization should be more supportive. Organizational support may be provided as simply as asking workers how they are doing or how their day is going. Managers can walk around and offer support by demonstrating availability. As one of the workers stated in this study, many times the managers are also seeing clients ... 'how do you interrupt managers from client work?'

Dattilio (2015) pointed out most mental-health workers prefer to evade seeking services for themselves because they fear embarrassment and anonymity. Other researchers demonstrated service provision is affected when the worker has become affected by either VT or STS (Dorociak et al., 2017; Knight, 2013; Sansbury et al., 2015).

Who is responsible for mental-health workers self-care ... the individual, the organization, or the governing boards? According to Packenham (2015), self-care is principally personal responsibility, but professional organizations, psychology accreditation bodies, and licensing boards have a part in the responsibility – or even a duty – in promoting self-care in the profession. It is important to promote wellness and self-care. Although the responsibility may be shifted from personal to organizations to accreditation bodies, everyone is responsible. Awareness needs to be bought to the phenomena, not only for the well-being of the people (patients, clients) served, but the well-being of the professional helpers.

Study Limitations

There were three-key limitations to this study. Limitations in research are influences beyond the researcher's control that may confine the outcomes expected by the researcher. The first limitation of this study was the researcher did not take the experience of the participants into account when selecting participants for the study. It is possible the inexperience of the participants who were not in the clinical workforce for a certain amount of time may have impacted their reporting of VT. The participants in this study ranged from less than a year to over 30

years of experience. It cannot be assumed that
mental-health workers with more experience shared
deeper accounts of lived experiences or that mental-
health workers with fewer years of experience shared
less. The results of this study demonstrate the STSS
score had no correlation to personal stories and
accounts shared by the research study participants.

The second limitation the study had was better
outcomes and understanding of VT could have been
obtained if a different methodology was used,
perhaps using a mixed-method study. A mixed-
method study may have allowed for the inclusion of a
larger sample; however, this would have limited the
qualitative component, as qualitative studies call for
smaller samples. The phenomenological approach
used as a method for this study allowed for the use of
the semi-structured interviews as a source to collect
rich descriptions of lived experiences. Due to the
methodology used in this study, the participants were
allowed to give deeper, denser responses that could
not have been captured using other methods. A
larger sample size would have made it difficult to use
interviews to gather data.

The third limitation was all of the participants in this study were females, which eliminated the male perspective. The only male interested in the study scored under a 28 on the STSS, which disqualified him from participating in the study. All steps were taken to minimize limitations; certain limitations in research are inherent (Bride, 2007).

Recommendations for Future Research

The type of method used to conduct this study on mental-health workers, VT, and self-care was a unique phenomenological approach. Although phenomenology has been used in other studies, it had not been used in search of the lived experiences associated with mental-health workers and their use of self-care. The outcomes derived from this study suggest a need for continued research. Although the findings allowed the research questions to be addressed, they also demonstrated the need for further research. The phenomenon of VT affects mental-health workers in different aspects, which leads to deeper and more complicated issues. As demonstrated by studies in the literature review,

VT/STS, affect different aspects of the mental-health workers life. Not only is VT/STS associated with job turn over, burnout, stress, anxiety and even sexual activities, it is also associated with deeper factors, such as a change in mental states and emotions. Future research should be focused on VT and its association with mental-health workers, especially in the areas of self-care. Although mental-health workers practice what they believe is self-care, there is no protocol or tool designed to administer self-care or to measure the positive or negative consequences of such care. Although previous studies have addressed this phenomenon and demonstrated the effects it has on mental-health workers and other helping professionals, there is no documentation on prevention, treatment, or management of VT.

The following are suggested changes to future research studies. It would be valuable to conduct studies in which both male and female perspectives are considered. This research study included only female participants, as the only male participant did not score over a 28 on the STSS, thus disqualifying him. Other studies should consider licensure and job responsibilities. There may be certain healthcare professionals more exposed to VT than others; for example, licensed professionals as opposed to unlicensed workers, case managers, or administrative staff.

It would be beneficial to conduct studies to determine if a specific discipline is more at risk than another. Is a licensed worker more exposed to VT than an unlicensed worker? Future research should include administrative office staff, as many times clients share information with them. This study incorporated a phenomenological approach, thereby limiting the sample size. A different approach, such as a mixed study, would allow for a larger sample size, thus allowing the outcomes to be generalized. Other recommendations are to conduct parallel studies using two mental health agencies, instead of one, and comparing the outcomes.

Conclusion

This research study adds to the body of knowledge by focusing on mental-health workers, VT, and self-care. Vicarious trauma denotes the cumulative effect of working with distressed clients, involving intrusion with the therapist's feelings, intellectual schemas, worldview recollections, self-efficacy, and sense of safety (Dorociak et al., 2017). Vicarious trauma does not reproduce illness in the therapist or the survivor; rather, VT is the transferring of traumatic stress by listening to the disturbing clinical material (Hernandez-Wolfe et al., 2015).

Mental-health professionals are exposed to VT daily. Through work, mental-health professionals are exposing themselves to additional trauma, which in turn can have lasting consequences that affects them … they may not be aware of the exposure to Vicarious Trauma that may even happening.

There is an increase in significance of self-care for mental-health workers and other specialists (Dorociak et al., 2017). The purpose of this study was to investigate mental-health workers' lived experiences of coping with VT and how they practice self-care. The research problem was that mental-health workers who experience vicarious trauma through daily work rarely practice self-care. The research question that guided this study was, "How do mental-health workers describe coping with vicarious trauma?" The research sub-question was,

"How do mental-health workers use self-care in response to vicarious trauma?"

This research study did answer the research questions. From the descriptions of lived experience shared by the workers, it was found mental-health workers have a few coping strategies which would effectively manage VT. All 12 of the mental-health workers had their own meaning of self-care; therefore, they adapted self-care techniques derived from their interpretations. Mental-health workers who did practice self-care did not do it daily, nor did they have a standard of self-care related to managing VT.

The results of this study provided new knowledge to assist mental-health workers in comprehending the need for self-care and assessing themselves for VT and STS. The study outcomes identified symptoms and feelings associated with trauma work through the lived experiences of mental-health workers. Mental-health workers, educators, and organizations are encouraged to seek strategies, management, and assessment of VT and STS. Organizations should promote the well-being of mental-health workers through adequate supervision and an organizational culture of care. Mental health organizations need to acknowledge and address the phenomenon to retain staff and improve the quality of service. This research project, if recommendations for training and self-care strategies are put into place, should result in higher job retention, a lower number of staff turnover, improved quality of care, and a better quality of life for mental-health workers. It will be advantageous to both professionals and organizations if VT is managed, identified, and treated with self-care initiatives and education.

Plan of Action

The results of this study were disseminated using a written report during a general staff meeting on October 19, 2018. As a result, the agency leadership scheduled an agency-wide training geared towards working with trauma. The training had a self-care component geared at the benefits of self-care while working with traumatized individuals and families. The Trauma Informed Trainings were a three-day, all-day event held on three consecutive Fridays. The training was provided by the Traumatic Stress Institute.

The administration voiced a concern for staff wellness and self-care by launching a Self-Care and Wellness Committee working towards implementing self-care activities during staff meetings and general staff meetings. Moving forward, the agency administration will be seeking ways in which to monitor STS on an ongoing basis, to ensure staff wellness and decrease staff turnover.

References

Aparicio, E., Michalopoulos, L.M., & Unick, G.J. (2013). An examination of the psychometric properties of the vicarious trauma scale in a sample of licensed social workers. *Health & Social Work, 38*(4), 199-206. doi:10.1093/hsw/hlt017

Ataria, Y. (2014). Traumatic memories as black holes: A qualitative-phenomenological approach. *Qualitative Psychology, 1*(2), 123-140. doi:10.1037/qup0000009

Baker, E.K. (2003a). Tending mind, body, and spirit. In *Caring for ourselves: A therapist's guide to personal and professional well-being* (pp. 59-97). Washington, DC: American Psychological Association. doi:10.1037/10482-004

Baker, E.K. (2003b). Therapist self-care needs across the lifespan. In *Caring for ourselves: A therapist's guide to personal and professional well-being* (pp. 25-35). Washington, DC: American Psychological Association. doi:10.1037/10482-002

Barnett, J.E., Baker, E.K., Elman, N.S., & Schoener, G.R. (2007). In pursuit of wellness: The self-care imperative. *Professional Psychology: Research and Practice, 38*(6), 603-612. doi:10.1037/0735-7028.38.6.603

Beaumont, E., Durkin, M., Hollins Martin, C.J., & Carson, J. (2016). Measuring relationships between self-compassion, compassion fatigue, burnout and well-being in student counselors and student cognitive behavioral psychotherapists: A quantitative survey. *Counselling & Psychotherapy Research, 16*(1), 15-23. doi:10.1002/capr.12054

Bell, C.H., & Robinson, E.H., III (2013). Shared trauma in counseling: Information and implications for counselors. *Journal of Mental Health Counseling, 35*(4), 310-323. doi:10.17744/mehc.35.4.7v33258020948502

Boulanger, G. (2016). When is vicarious trauma a necessary therapeutic tool? *Psychoanalytic Psychology, 35*(1), 60-69. doi:10.1037/pap0000089

Branson, D.C., Weigand, D.A., & Keller, J.E. (2014). Vicarious trauma and decreased sexual desire: A hidden hazard of helping others. *Psychological Trauma: Theory, Research, Practice, and Policy, 6*(4), 398-403. doi:10.1037/a0033113

Bride, B.E. (2007). Prevalence of secondary traumatic stress among social workers. *Social Work, 52*(1), 63-70.

https://doi.org/10.1093/sw/52.1.63

Bride, B.E. & Kintzle, S. (2011). Secondary traumatic stress, job satisfaction, and occupational commitment in substance abuse counselors. *Traumatology, 17*(1), 22-28. doi:10.1177/1534765610395617

Bride, B., Robinson, M., Yegidis, B., & Figley, C. (2004). Development and validation of the secondary traumatic stress scale. *Research on Social Work Practice, 14*(1), 27-35. doi:10.1177/1049731503254106.

Brockhouse, R., Msetfi, R. M., Cohen, K., & Joseph, S. (2011). Vicarious exposure to trauma and growth in therapists: The moderating effects of sense of coherence, organizational support, and empathy. *Journal of Traumatic Stress, 24*(6), 735-742. doi:10.1002/jts.20704

Butler, L.D., Carello, J., & Maguin, E. (2017). Trauma, stress, and self-care in clinical training: Predictors of burnout, decline in health status, secondary traumatic stress symptoms, and compassion satisfaction. *Psychological Trauma: Theory, Research, Practice, and Policy, 9*(4), 416-424. doi:10.1037/tra0000187

Caringi, J.C., Hardiman, E.R., Weldon, P., Fletcher, S., Devlin, M., & Stanick, C. (2017). Secondary traumatic stress and licensed clinical social workers. *Traumatology, 23*(2), 186-195. doi:10.1037/trm0000061

Cetrano, G., Tedeschi, F., Rabbi, L., Gosetti, G., Lora, A., Lamonaca, D., ... Amaddeo, Francesco. (2017). How are compassion fatigue, burnout, and compassion satisfaction affected by quality of working life? Findings from a survey of mental health staff in Italy. *BMC Health Services Research, 17*(1). doi:10.1186/s12913-017-2726-x

Choi, G.Y. (2011) Organizational impacts on the secondary traumatic stress of social workers assisting family violence or sexual assault survivors, *Administration in Social Work, 35*(3), 225-242, doi: 10.1080/03643107.2011.575333

Cleary, M., Horsfall, J., & Hayter, M. (2014). Data collection and sampling in qualitative research: Does size matter? *Journal of Advanced Nursing, 70*(3), 473-475. doi:10.1111/jan.12163

Connally, D. (2012). The relationship between clinician sex, ethnicity, sexual identity, and secondary traumatic stress. *Journal of Gay & Lesbian Mental Health, 16*(4), 306-321. doi:10.1080/19359705.2012.697002

Cook, J.M., Simiola, V., Ellis, A.E., & Thompson, R. (2017). Training in trauma psychology: A national survey of doctoral graduate programs. *Training and Education in Professional Psychology, 11*(2), 108-114. doi:10.1037/tep0000150

Cox, K. & Steiner, S. (2013). Preserving commitment to social work service through the prevention of vicarious trauma. *Journal of Social Work Values & Ethics, 10*(1), 52-60. Retrieved from http://jswve.org/download/2013-1/articles(2)/52-52-Preserving%20Committment%20to%20Social%20Work%20Service.p

df
Dattilio, F.M. (2015). The self-care of psychologists and mental-health professionals: A review and practitioner guide. *Australian Psychologist, 50*(6), 393-399. doi:10.1111/ap.12157
Day, K.W., Lawson, G. & Burge, P. (2017). Clinicians' experiences of shared trauma after the shootings at Virginia Tech. *Journal of Counseling & Development, 95*(3), 269-278. doi:10.1002/jcad.12141
Dombo, E.A. & Gray, C. (2013). Engaging spirituality in addressing vicarious trauma in clinical social workers: A self-care model. *Social Work & Christianity, 40*(1), 89-104. Retrieved from http://connection.ebscohost.com/c/articles/85443979/engaging -spirituality-addressing-vicarious-trauma-clinical-social-workers-self-care-model
Donalek, J.G. (2004). Phenomenology as a qualitative research method. *Urologic Nursing, 24*(6), 516-517. Retrieved from https://www.suna.org/sites/default/files/download/ members/unjarticles/2004/04dec/516.pdf
Doody, O. & Noonan, M. (2013). Preparing and conducting interviews to collect data. *Nurse Researcher, 20*(5), 28-32. doi.org/10.7748/nr2013.05.20.5.28. e 327
Dorociak, K.E., Rupert, P.A., Bryant, F.B., & Zahniser, E. (2017a). Development of the professional self-care scale. *Journal of Counseling Psychology, 64*(3), 325-334. doi:10.1037/cou0000206
Dorociak, K.E., Rupert, P.A., & Zahniser, E. (2017b). Work life, well-being, and self-care across the professional lifespan of psychologists. *Professional Psychology: Research and Practice, 48*(6), 429-437. doi:10.1037/pro0000160
Dunkley, J. & Whelan, T.A. (2006). Vicarious traumatization: Current status and future directions. *British Journal of Guidance & Counselling, 34*(1), 107-116. doi:10.1080/03069880500483166
Edelkott, N., Engstrom, D.W., Hernandez-Wolfe, P., & Gangsei, D. (2016). Vicarious resilience: Complexities and variations. *American Journal of Orthopsychiatry, 86*(6), 713-724. doi:10.1037/ort0000180
Ellis, P. (2016). The language of research (part 8): Phenomenological research. *Wounds UK, 12*(1), 128-129. Retrieved from https://www.wounds-uk.com/download/resource/931
Figley, C.R. (1999). Compassion fatigue: Toward a new understanding of the costs of caring. In B. H. Stamm (Ed.), *Secondary traumatic stress: Self-care issues for clinicians, researchers, and educators* (pp. 3-28). Baltimore, MD: Sidran Press.
Figley, C.R. (1995). *Brunner/Mazel psychological stress series, No. 23. Compassion fatigue: Coping with secondary traumatic stress disorder in those who treat the traumatized.* Philadelphia, PA: Brunner/Mazel.
Finklestein, M., Stein, E., Greene, T., Bronstein, I., & Solomon, Z. (2015). Posttraumatic stress disorder and vicarious trauma in

mental-health professionals. *Health & Social Work, 40*(2), e25-e31. doi:10.1093/hsw/hlv026

Goodwin, M. & Richards, K. (2017). Best practices in healthcare management begin with self-care. *Nursing Economics, 35*(3), 152-155. Retrieved from from http://www.self-careacademy.com/PDFs/bestbractices-healthcaremanagment.pdf

Hacker, K. (2013). *Community-based participatory research.* Thousand Oaks, CA: Sage Publications.

Halevi, E. & Idisis, Y. (2017). Who helps the helper? Differentiation of self as an indicator for resisting vicarious traumatization. *Psychological Trauma: Theory, Research, Practice, and Policy.* doi:10.1037/tra0000318

Hernandez-Wolfe, P., Killian, K., Engstrom, D., & Gangsei, D. (2015). Vicarious resilience, vicarious trauma, and awareness of equity in trauma work. *Journal of Humanistic Psychology, 55*(2), 153-172. doi:10.1177/0022167814534322

Hyatt-Burkhart, D. (2014). The experience of vicarious posttraumatic growth in mental-health workers. *Journal of Loss and Trauma, 19*(5), 452-461. doi:10.1080/15325024.2013.797268

Ivicic, R., & Motta, R. (2017). Variables associated with secondary traumatic stress among mental-health professionals. *Traumatology, 23*(2), 196-204. doi:10.1037/trm0000065

Kintzle, S., Yarvis, J.S., & Bride, B.E. (2013). Secondary traumatic stress in military primary and mental health care providers. *Military Medicine, 178*(12), 1310-1315. doi:10.7205/MILMED-D-13-00087

Kirkwood, A. & Price, L. (2013). Examining some assumptions and limitations of research on the effects of emerging technologies for teaching and learning in higher education. *British Journal of Educational Technology, 44*(4), 536-543. doi:10.1111/bjet.12049

Knight, C. (2013). Indirect trauma: Implications for self-care, supervision, the organization, and the academic institution. *The Clinical Supervisor, 32*(2), 224-243. doi:10.1080/07325223.2013.850139

Kulkarni, S., Bell, H., Hartman, J.L., & Herman-Smith, R. (2013). Exploring individual and organizational factors contributing to compassion satisfaction, secondary traumatic stress, and burnout in domestic violence service providers. *Journal of the Society for Social Work & Research, 4*(2), 114-130. doi:10.5243/jsswr.2013.8

Lester, S. (1999). An Introduction to phenomenological research. Taunton UK. Retrieved from http:/www.sld.demon.co.uk/resmethy.pdf

Looney, T.L. (2016). *Small business owner's recession experiences: A qualitative phenomenological study* (Doctoral dissertation, University of Phoenix).

Mairean, C. & Turliuc, M.N. (2013). Predictors of vicarious trauma beliefs among medical staff. *Journal of Loss & Trauma, 18*(5), 414-428. doi:10.1080/15325024.2012.714200

Marshall, C. & Rossman, G.B. (2011). *Designing qualitative research.*

Thousand Oaks, CA: Sage Publications.

McCann, I.L. & Pearlman, L.A. (1990a). *Psychological trauma and the adult survivor: Theory, therapy, and transformation.* Philadelphia, PA: Brunner/Mazel.

McCann, I.L. & Pearlman, L.A. (1990b). Vicarious traumatization: A framework for understanding the psychological effects of working with victims. *Journal of Traumatic Stress, 3*(1), 131-149. https://doi.org/10.1002/jts.2490030110

McCormack, L. & Adams, E.L. (2016). Therapists, complex trauma, and the medical model: Making meaning of vicarious distress from complex trauma in the inpatient setting. *Traumatology, 22*(3), 192-202. doi:10.1037/trm0000024

McDavid, J.C., Huse, I., & Hawthorn, L.R. (2013). *Program evaluation and performance measurement: An introduction to practice* (2nd ed.). Thousand Oaks, CA: Sage Publications.

McNiff, J. (2017). *Action research: All you need to know.* Thousand Oaks, CA: Sage Publications.

Middleton, J.S. & Potter, C.C. (2015). The relationship between vicarious traumatization and turnover among child welfare professionals. *Journal of Public Child Welfare, 9*(2), 195-216. doi:10.1080/15548732.2015.1021987

Molnar, B.E., Sprang, G., Killian, K.D., Gottfried, R., Emery, V., & Bride, B.E. (2017). Advancing science and practice for vicarious traumatization/secondary traumatic stress: A research agenda. *Traumatology, 23*(2), 129-142. doi:10.1037/trm0000122

Moustakas, C.E. (1994). *Phenomenological research methods.* Thousand Oaks, CA: Sage Publications, Inc.

National Association of Social Workers [NASW]. (2017). Code of Ethics: Retrieved from https://www.socialworkers.org/About/Ethics/Code-of-Ethics

Newell, J.M. & Nelson-Gardell, D. (2014). A competency-based approach to teaching professional self-care: An ethical consideration for social work educators. *Journal of Social Work Education, 50*(3), 427-439. doi:10.1080/10437797.2014.917928

Norcross, J.C. & Guy, J.D. (2007). *Leaving it at the office: A guide to psychotherapist self-care.* New York City, NY: Guilford Press.

Pakenham, K.I. (2015). Comment on "the self-care of psychologists and mental-health professionals". *Australian Psychologist, 50*(6), 405-408. doi:10.1111/ap.12145

Pearlman, L.A. (1995). Self-care for trauma therapists: Ameliorating vicarious traumatization. In B. H. Stamm (Ed.), *Secondary traumatic stress: Self-care issues for clinicians, researchers, and educators* (pp. 51-64). Baltimore, MD: The Sidran Press. Retrieved from http://psycnet.apa.org/record/1996-97172-004

Pearlman, L.A. & Maclan, P.S. (1995). Vicarious traumatization: An empirical study of the effects of trauma work on trauma therapists. *Professional Psychology: Research and Practice, 26*(6), 558-565. doi:10.1037/0735-7028.26.6.558

Pearlman, L.A. & Saakvitne, K.W. (1995a). *Trauma and the therapist: Countertransference and vicarious traumatization in psychotherapy with incest survivors.* New York City, NY: W.W. Norton & Company.

Pearlman, L.A. & Saakvitne, K.W. (1995b). Treating therapists with vicarious traumatization and secondary traumatic stress disorders. In C. Figley (Ed.), *Compassion fatigue: Coping with secondary traumatic stress disorder in those who treat the traumatized* (pp. 150-177). New York City, NY: Brunner/Mazel.

Petrovich, J.C. & Cronley, C.C. (2015). Deep in the heart of Texas: A phenomenological exploration of unsheltered homelessness. *American Journal of Orthopsychiatry, 85*(4), 315-323. doi:10.1037/ort0000043

Pryce, J.G., Shackelford, K.K., & Pryce, D.H. (2007). *Secondary traumatic stress and the child welfare professional.* Chicago: Lyceum Books.

QSR International. (2014). *Features and Benefits.* Retrieved from http://www.qsrinternational.com/products_nvivo-mac_features-and-benefits.aspx

QSR International.com. (2014). *What is Qualitative Research?* Retrieved from http://www.qsrinternational.com/what-is-qualitative-research.aspx

Runyan, C.N. (2017). "Joy" in practice requires workforce well-being. *Families, Systems, & Health, 35*(4), 513-514. doi:10.1037/fsh0000319

Rzeszutek, M., Partyka, M., & Golab, A. (2015). Temperament traits, social support, and secondary traumatic stress disorder symptoms in a sample of trauma therapists. *Professional Psychology: Research and Practice, 46*(4), 213-220. doi:10.1037/pro0000024

Saakvitne, K.W., Tennen, H., & Affleck, G. (1998). Exploring thriving in the context of clinical trauma theory: Constructivist self-development theory. *Journal of Social Issues, 54*(2), 279-299. doi.org/10.1111/0022-4537.661998066

Saldaña, J. (2016). *The coding manual for qualitative researchers.* Los Angeles, CA: Sage. http://www.worldcat.org/title/coding-manual-for-qualitative-researchers/oclc/930445694

Sansbury, B.S., Graves, K., & Scott, W. (2015). Managing traumatic stress responses among clinicians: Individual and organizational tools for self-care. *Trauma, 17*(2), 114-122. doi:10.1177/1460408614551978

Santana, M.C. & Fouad, N.A. (2017). Development and validation of a self-care behavior inventory. *Training and Education in Professional Psychology, 11*(3), 140-145. doi:10.1037/tep0000142

Shannon, P.J., Simmelink-McCleary, J., Im, H., Becher, E., & Crook-Lyon, R. (2014). Developing self-care practices in a trauma treatment course. *Journal of Social Work Education, 50*(3), 440-453. doi:10.1080/10437797.2014.91793

Shannonhouse, L., Barden, S., Jones, E., Gonzalez, L., & Murphy, A.

(2016). Secondary traumatic stress for trauma researchers: A mixed methods research design. *Journal of Mental Health Counseling, 38*(3), 201-216. doi:10.1774/mehc.38.3.02

Sheehan, S. (2014). A conceptual framework for understanding transcendental phenomenology through the lived experiences of biblical leaders. *Emerging Leadership Journeys, 7*(1), 10-20.

Shively, R. (2017). Burnout: Managing staff burnout and vicarious trauma in the workplace. *Corrections Today, 79*(6), 44-91. Retrieved from http://www.aca.org/ACA_Prod_IMIS/ DOCS/Corrections%20Today/2017%20Articles/November%202017 /CT-Nov-Dec%202017_Burnout.pdf

Swanson, R.A. & Holton, I. (2005). *Research in organizations: Foundations and methods of inquiry.* Oakland, CA: Berrett-Koehler Publishers.

Tavormina, M. & Clossey, L. (2015). Exploring crisis and its effects on workers in child protective services work. *Child & Family Social Work, 22*(1), 126-136. doi:10.1111/cfs.12209

Thompson, I.A., Amatea, E.S., & Thompson, E.S. (2014). Personal and contextual predictors of mental health counselors' compassion fatigue and burnout. *Journal of Mental Health Counseling, 36*(1), 58-77. doi.org/10.17744/mehc.36.1.p61m73373m4617r3

Vaughn, P. & Turner, C. (2015). Decoding via coding: Analyzing qualitative text data through thematic coding and survey methodologies. *Journal of Library Administration, 56*(1), 41-51. doi:10.1080/01930826.2015.1105035

Wagaman, M.A., Geiger, J.M., Shockley, C., & Segal, E.A. (2015). The role of empathy in burnout, compassion satisfaction, and secondary traumatic stress among social workers. *Social Work, 60*(3), 201-209. doi:10.1093/SW/swv014

Wheeler, D.P. & McClain, A. (2015). *Social work speaks: National Association of Social Workers policy statements, 2015-2017* (10th ed.). Washington, DC: NASW Press.

Wise, E.H., Hersh, M.A., & Gibson, C.M. (2012). Ethics, self-care, and well-being for psychologists: Re-envisioning the stress-distress continuum. *Professional Psychology: Research and Practice, 43*(5), 487-494. doi:10.1037/a0029446

Yazdani, A. & Shafi, K. (2014). Indirect exposure to violence and prevalence of vicarious trauma in adolescents. *Bahria Journal of Professional Psychology, 13*(2), 57-71.

Zahniser, E., Rupert, P.A., & Dorociak, K.E. (2017). Self-care in clinical psychology graduate training. *Training and Education in Professional Psychology, 11*(4), 283-289. doi:10.1037/tep0000172

Appendix

Interview Guide

1. Describe your experience at work as a mental-health worker (Answers Research Question)

2. Describe ways in which your job causes you stress or anxiety, and how do you handle it (Answers Research Question)

3. Describe any physical symptoms that you experience during your day at work, or before starting your day of work, and how do you cope with them. (Answers Research Question)

4. Describe your experience as a mental-health worker when you continue to think of a situation at work after your day of work has ended. (Answers Research Question)

5. Describe an experience where you identify with a client/patient and their presenting issues. (Answers Research Question)

6. Describe feelings of inadequacy at work. (Answers Research question)

7. Describe any support systems you may have available at work if you experience anxiety or stress. (Answers Sub-Question)

8. Describe what self-care means to you. (Answers Sub-Question)

9. Describe activities that you engage in that lead to self-care. (Answers Sub-Question)

10. Describe ways in which your place of work supports or promotes self-care. Do you have any suggestions for improving these activities? (Answers Sub-Question)

Index

Curriculum Vitae

Dr. Soraya Martinez Sawicki, L.C.S.W.
MSW, LMSW, LSW
Farmington, CT 06032
(860) 986-1287 / sorayasawicki@aol.com

EXPERIENCE SUMMARY

- 16+ years, Director / Supervising Manager (Mental Health Clinical Services)
- 17+ years, Counselor (Mental Health Services)
- 4 years, Entrepreneur / Business Manager (Mental and Physical Health Services)

EXPERIENCE PORTFOLIO

10/16 – present, Owner
Mental Health and Holistic Services
Infinity Integrated Counseling and Spa Services LLC., Farmington, CT

- Supervise staff of three clinicians, three massage, and reiki practitioners, volunteers and interns, as well as training and development to company procedures, policies, and standards
- Seeing patients six days a week

- Perform business development and marketing of the business Website, Facebook, Community Presentations
- Liaise with insurance services, including: Medicaid, Medicare, Anthem, United Health, Tri-Care, Cigna and Aetna;
- Manage daily operations; responsible for bookkeeping services, data payroll company, invoicing, and supply inventory

02/15 – 11/16, Program Director
Behavioral Health Home
Community Health Resources, Manchester, CT

- Oversaw program operations, quality outcomes and attainment of program goals
- Provided leadership to the implementation and coordination of care and services.
- Designed and developed administrative and clinical policies and procedures
- Monitored and reported performance, outcomes and leads quality improvement efforts
- Provided training, clinical consultation, case planning, coordination and general
- Provided comprehensive care management, care coordination, health promotion, comprehensive transitional care, patient and family support, and referrals to community support services
- Worked to improve medical and behavioral health care coordination to clients
- Worked to reduce healthcare disparities
- Developed / maintained relationships with primary- and specialty-care providers including inpatient facilities

- Worked with internal and external providers and promoted coordination of activities
- Maintained client and staff records
- Timely completion of reports and performance indicators

04/14 – 01/15, Program Director
Catholic Charities
Institute for the Hispanic Families, Hartford, CT

- Planned the delivery of overall program and activities to achieve mission and goals of the organization; developed new initiatives to support the strategic direction of the organization
- Developed and implemented long-term goals and objectives; developed an annual budget and operating plan to support program within the approved budget
- Developed a program evaluation framework to assess the strengths of the program and to identify areas for improvement
- Assisted the site Director in developing funding proposals for the program to ensure the continuous delivery of services; developed forms / records to document program activities
- Ensured program activities operated within the policies and procedures of the organization and complied with all relevant legislation and professional standards
- Oversaw the collection and maintenance of records on the clients of the program for statistical purposes according to the confidentiality/privacy policy of the organization
- Recruited, interviewed and selected qualified program staff in consultation with Site Director

- Implemented human resources policies, procedures, and practices; including personnel files for program; established / implemented performance management process for staff
- Communicated with funders as outlined in funding agreements and ensured reports and supporting documentation were prepared as outlined
- Monitored and approved all budgeted program expenditures
- Identified and evaluated the risks associated with program activities and took appropriate action to control the risks
- Monitored the program activities on a regular basis and conducted an annual staff evaluation according to the program evaluation framework
- Reported evaluation findings to the Site Director and recommended changes to enhance the program, as appropriate
- Conducted internal audits; supervised case management programs and support staff
- Coordinated MSW Internship programs with St Joseph College

04/13 – 03/14, Assistant Director
Family Reunification Program
Lincoln Hall, Lincolndale, NY

- Supervised Lead Clinicians. Lead Case Managers, Release Coordinators, and Administrative staff
- Coordinated both programmatic and financial elements of the services, including Family Reunification Program's overall outcomes; acting secondary liaison to the Office of Refugee Resettlement to provide to the UAC in care

- Assisted Director with analyzing program needs; participated in management meetings
- Worked with other agency staff and regulatory agencies to develop long-term planning and policy development to ensure compliance with federal state and local regulations
- Approved outgoing assessments, case summaries, and treatment plans
- Maintained communication with Department of Homeland Security and Immigrations Custom Enforcement (ICE)

02/09 – 03/13, Director of Operations
Psychotherapist
CitiCare, Inc., New York, NY

- Managed departments, receiving reports, commutations, requests for aid and the like from all managers, in the first instance, and from any employees
- Ensured daily operations of all programs, clinical and mental health
- Supervised nursing, social work, and clinical directors, maintenance, administrative, and case managing staff
- Provided resources for in-services to staff with guidance from leadership
- Supervised preparation and execution of audit operations relating to Operations / Support Departments, receiving close interaction with relevant department managers
- Liaised with managed care HMO's, Medicaid, Medicare, Affinity, Blue Cross Blue Shield, and Metro-Plus insurance providers

- Collaborated with Department of Mental Health and Office of Mental Health
- Provided psychotherapy to chronically mentally ill individuals, family, and children; worked closely with severely and persistently mentally ill, re-entry from prison, foster care, the elderly, and other special populations; conducted group therapy, psychosocial assessments, and applied correct diagnosis according to DSM-IV
- Initiated Social Services department - Housing, SSI, HRA 2OIOEs, worked with residential, SROs, DOH, level I, 11,111, and shelter sits
- Assured all staff were following clinical and best practice, policies and procedures
- Evaluated patient complaints; evaluated provider service through initial, three months, six months, and yearly evaluations
- Assured treatment plans and goals met; assured patients had basic needs; worked with case managers, doctors and psychiatrists; assured patients are medication compliant, consulted with all parties to ensure treatment followed, needs were met, and patients were receiving appropriate levels of care
- Developed the social work component for the clinic and established the need for social services as one of the most important factors in establishing and maintaining better health and mental health

01/05 – 01/10, Program Director
Weston United Act Team, New York, NY

- Actively participated in the development and implementation of program policies and procedures

- Ensured contract compliance with standards established by the agency
- Oversaw all aspects of management at the clinical and administrative level; performed evaluation and weekly supervision for a professional team
- Attended meetings with Office of Mental Health.
- Provided, created and monitored all quality improvement systems to ensure that all chart documentation and contract requirements were up to date
- Recruited, oriented, promoted and disciplined staff; conducted staff performance evaluations, in-service education, training, and weekly supervision of staff
- Accompanied staff to visit community consumers to offer tips and advice on engaging mental illness with various proven strategies and methods
- Quality assured / submitted fiscal reports and CAIRS Data; oversaw program finances and monitored transactions

02/05 – 02/08, Director of Preventive Services Administrative Clinical Supervisor Community Association of Progressive Dominicans, Inc., New York, NY

- Managed administration and oversight of Audubon Youth Program (AYP) and OCFS (Adolescent Pregnancy Preventive Services) APPS Program, including management of contracts with subcontracting agencies
- Established and maintained systems for documenting services and for the maintenance of client records; provided necessary reports and recorded statistics as required

*Mental Health Workers' Vicarious Trauma,
Secondary Traumatic Stress, and Self-Care*

- Implemented clinical supervision of clinical APPS and AYP staff and for in-service training; participated as member of Outpatient Mental Health interdisciplinary team
- Represented the Department/Agency at community meetings, conferences, workshops, seminars, and ACDP's inter-department meetings
- Worked with Department Director in program development and planning, including grants and proposals
- Ensured program compliance with regulations, standards, and codes at state level.
- Participated in hiring, evaluating and termination of program staff; supervised Masters-level, social-work interns
- Provided short- or long-term psychotherapy services to children, adolescents, and adults within the treatment modalities of individual, group, couples, or family treatment, dealing with sexual abuse, domestic violence, problem behavior, and anger management; carried an active caseload of clients as stipulated by Department of Family and Clinical Services

02/03 – 01/05, Clinical Supervisor
Alianza Dominicana, Inc., New York, NY

- Supervised five full-time clinicians, seven fee-for-service clinicians and Master of Social Work interns responsible for servicing patients; maintained network with referral sources
- Enacted quality improvement projects for Mental Health Clinic / Ryan White Contracts
- Participated in writing/revising policy and procedures

- Carried a caseload of 20+ participants to include HIV positive individuals, domestic violence victims, sexual abuse victims and abused children
- Organized adolescent educational support groups
- Coordinated training, agency meetings, committees, special projects, conferences and parades

02/00 – 01/03, Program Supervisor
Alianza Dominicana, Inc., New York, NY

- Supervised five family support workers and assigned cases
- Wrote program reports and completed psychosocial assessments
- Scheduled and provided orientation for new employees

01/00 – 11/00, Counselor
Hope Program Mental Health Workers, New York, NY

- Provided individual counseling for HIV+ participants, homeless and domestic violence victims; conducted program intakes and assessments

01/99 – 12/99, Social Worker / Case Worker
Salvation Army, New York, NY

- Provided social services for children/foster home and adoption services
- Provided biological parents with referrals and counseling for drug treatment, domestic violence issues and anger management

- Provided home visits and completed uniform case reports
- Provided court appearances on behalf of the Salvation Army and the Clients

FORMAL EDUCATION

- 2019, Doctoral of Social Work, Public Service Leadership, Capella University, Minneapolis, MN
- 2003, Master of Social Work, Yeshiva University, New York, NY
- 1999, Bachelor of Arts, Psychology, City College of New York, New York, NY

CAREER TRAINING / CERTIFICATIONS

- Licensed Clinical Social Worker, New York
- Licensed Clinical Social Worker, Connecticut
- Certified Clinical Trauma Professional, Connecticut
- 2005 – present Certificate, SIFI-Seminar for Field Instruction, Fordham University, New York, NY

TECHNICAL / LANGUAGES / TRADE ORGANIZATIONS

- MS Office: Word, Excel, PowerPoint, Outlook
- Therapy Notes Electronic Health records
- PSDCRS Database
- CDCS Database
- Bilingual - Spanish/English
- 2002 - present, Member, National Association of Social Workers, Boston, AM

About the Author

Dr. Sawicki is a trained psychotherapist who has dedicated over 20 years of service to the field of Social Work. She graduated from Capella University with a Doctor of Social Work, and Yeshiva University's Wurzweiler School of Social Work with her Masters' Degree in Clinical Studies. She provides services to populations in Connecticut and New York, in her private practice, as well as virtually.

She founded Infinity Integrated Counseling and Spa Services, LLC in 2015. Dr. Sawicki created Infinity with the idea that lives can be renewed through holistic, integrated practices that help heal the mind, body, and spirit. Infinity is a safe, inviting space that is a sanctuary for relaxation and personal growth.

Dr. Sawicki is a subject matter expert in trauma work and specializes in anxiety, depression, and cultural issues. Her dissertation was on vicarious trauma and secondary traumatic stress. Soraya works with individuals regarding different life issues; however, found that working with individuals regarding personal issues and how it interferes with the professional aspect of their life has been the most rewarding.

Soraya is a resident of Connecticut, practices psychotherapy in her private practice, and provides online therapy through Thera-platform, while she continues to work on other social and private projects.

Dr. Sawicki lives in Connecticut with her husband and is the mother of five children.

Social Media

Email Address:

soravasawicki@aol.com

Infinity Integrated Counseling and Spa
offers licensed counseling with the integration of
a variety of specialized holistic services.
35 Tower Lane, Avon, Connecticut
(860) 404-2736

Business Website:

http://infinity-integrated.com/

Business Facebook Page:

https://www.facebook.com/Infini
tyIntegrated/

About the Book

This is a 'must-buy book' for mental-health workers, licensed social workers, licensed professional counselors, and licensed marriage and family therapists, and/or the organizations for who these helpers work. This books' research study focuses on keeping the helping work-force mentally and emotionally stable after encountering second-hand trauma from their clients or patients. First responders, social workers, and mental health professionals encounter experiences directly or indirectly through helping others in emergencies, following trauma care, and/or mental health care treatments. While these workers help others, they may also experience vicarious trauma or 're-experience' past traumas of their own as they are re-lived via their patients or clients.

The researcher identifies care of symptoms presented by mental-health workers, licensed social workers, licensed professional counselors, and licensed marriage and family therapists who are exposed to and may suffer VT/STS from their clients. This study documents how some social workers treat their own mental, emotional, and physical VT symptoms with 'self-care,' as well as how their supervisors can acknowledge and provide support directly to the mental health professionals to reduce or alleviate VT/STS.

Made in the USA
Las Vegas, NV
12 September 2021